The Social Thought of Thomas Merton

The Way of Nonviolence and Peace for the Future

by David W. Givey

FRANCISCAN HERALD PRESS
1434 WEST 51st STREET • CHICAGO, 60609

Library of Congress Cataloging in Publication Data

Givey, David W.
The social thought of Thomas Merton.

Includes bibliographical references.
1. Nonviolence—Religious aspects—Christianity—History—20th century.   2. Merton, Thomas, 1915–1968.
I. Title.
BT736.6.G58   1983   261.8'092'4   83-1646
ISBN 0-8199-0859-2

Nihil Obstat: Rev. Msgr. James McGrath, J.C.D.
Censor Librorum

Imprimatur: John Cardinal Krol, J.C.D., D.D.
Archbishop of Philadelphia
August 13, 1982

The Nihil Obstat and Imprimatur are official declarations that a book or pamphlet is free of doctrinal or moral error. No implication is contained therein that those who have granted the Nihil Obstat or Imprimatur agree with the contents, opinions or statements expressed.

MADE IN THE UNITED STATES OF AMERICA

TO MY MOTHER († NOVEMBER 29, 1976)
WHO HAS TAUGHT ME BY THE WITNESS OF HER
LIFE, NOT ONLY WHAT IT MEANS TO BE A
CHRISTIAN, BUT HOW TO LIVE AT
PEACE IN THE WORLD.

AΩ

Acknowledgments

I would like to extend my sincere gratitude to His Eminence John Cardinal Krol, Archbishop of Philadelphia, not only for the Epilogue to this book, but for his faith, trust and support in the years of my research and study for this project; to Msgr. John Tracy Ellis for his guidance and encouragement and for writing the Forward; to Brother Patrick Hart, Thomas Merton's secretary, for sharing his personal insights and recollections and for contributing the Prologue.

My heart-felt appreciation goes to my mother, my best friend and greatest source of inspiration and optimism; to my father who is the most peace-loving person I have ever known; to my step-mother who has added a new dimension to my life; to my brother Pat and his wife Mary who have been a constant source of joy and love; to my brother-priests the Reverends Daniel D. Doyle, M.Div., Edwin F. O'Brien S.T.D., Michael J. Bransfield, M.A., Donald H. Henry, M.Div., and Sherman W. Gray, S.S.L., who never let me give up; to Srs. Mary Terence and Kathleen Leary S.S.J., for typing, duplicating, and always smiling; and to all my wonderful friends and students for their understanding and love, and for constantly reminding me that I should try to practice what I preach and teach.

D.W.G.

Contents

Prologue

To many of his readers, Thomas Merton's critical and outspoken writings on social events in the late fifties and early sixties came undoubtedly as something of a surprise if not a shock. What was this cloistered contemplative monk up to? Should he not be attending to his prayers and his solitary life before the Lord, and not getting involved in social issues?

As Abbot John Eudes Bamberger noted in an essay which appeared some years ago,[1] the monks of Gethsemani were not unduly surprised by the emergence of Thomas Merton as a social critic and commentator, since he had been practicing for years, first of all on himself—he was his own severest critic—and then on the community of Gethsemani and the Order to which he belonged. But it was always a positive form of criticism.

His criticism in the early 1960s was directed primarily against the injustice meted out to minority groups of our nation, especially the Blacks and native Americans. His early critique was equally leveled at the two great power blocks, against capitalistic as well as communistic abuses of human rights and freedom. His penetrating "Letter to Pablo Antonio Cuadra Concerning Giants" was a good example of his social concern in this area.

With the United States' involvement in the Vietnam War, Merton spoke out strongly and courageously, even though it was at this time an unpopular cause. His plea was to make peace, not war. Merton also believed that the monk's essential role in society was his "prophetic function." As the early monks fled the evils of the ancient cities for the desert solitudes of Egypt as a refusal to condone the social standards of their day, so likewise the monks of our day have a duty to identify with movements of peace, and when occasion arises, to denounce all war-promoting initiatives. He felt monks must exercise their prophetic vocation above all by the witness of their lives of peace and harmony. In his own case, admittedly exceptional, Merton felt compelled in conscience to speak out against such evils—especially in regard to nuclear warfare, the stockpiling of nuclear weapons, the arms race, and social injustices of all kinds. This was all the more true in a world where the rich get richer and the poor become poorer in the Third World nations.

Instead of being a contradiction in terms of the contemplative monastic life, Merton was convinced that an identification with the poor and alienated members of society was the duty of monks, and flowed quite naturally from living out the Gospel message. Since monks are simply a community of believers, who live the Gospel in a certain radical way, he felt deeply that they should above all espouse movements of peace and justice. Merton's pioneering efforts in this regard gradually affected other religious communities and eventually the entire Church in America. However, for a time Merton was forbidden by the Trappist Abbot General in Rome to write about nuclear warfare, but after Pope John XXIII's encyclical, *Pacem in Terris* was promulgated, the ban was lifted.

As this excellent study of Thomas Merton's philosophy of nonviolence by Fr. David Givey demonstrates, although not a total pacifist (he did believe a person or a country had the right to defend itself against an aggressor with conventional weapons), Merton was certainly a "nuclear pacifist," and was dedicated wholeheartedly to nonviolence as the only way of achieving peace. There was no possibility of "winning" a nuclear war.

Some social activists have indicated publicly that had Merton lived he would have given up his ideals of nonviolence and would have joined hands with guerrilla revolutionary groups in an attempt to overthrow unjust governments. Since Merton is not alive to defend himself on such speculation, or to clarify his position, I believe this carefully thoughtout work by Fr. Givey makes it obvious that there was a consistency in Merton's thinking on the subject of nonviolence as the only way to true and lasting peace.

The author has rendered a tremendous service in pointing out to us Merton's dedication of a philosophy of nonviolence at this particular moment in history. May his words be a source of encouragement to us all, so that we will continue to say ''No'' to the nuclear armament race, and ''Yes'' to a greater reliance on nonviolence as the only viable means of achieving peace in our times.

Brother Patrick Hart
Abbey of Gethsemani

Foreword

> If I have written about interracial justice, or thermonuclear
> weapons, it is because these issues are terribly relevant to
> one great truth: that man is called to live as a son of God.
> Man must respond to this call to live in peace with all his
> brothers in the One Christ.[1]

These words of Thomas Merton were written in connection with the
deposit of his papers at Bellarmine College in Louisville, Kentucky.
That interracial justice and thermonuclear weapons have not ceased to
be "terribly relevant," every thoughtful person will agree. Scarcely a
week passes that their relevance for the public mind is not renewed, and
that often in a way that threatens violence if, indeed, it does not induce
it. The subject of Father Givey's book is, then, itself highly relevant,
for the tempo of world violence has notably increased since the famous
monk met an accidental death in far off Bangkok near the end of the
fateful year of 1968. I say "fateful," for historians are likely to high-
light 1968 as one of the most anguished in recent American history. The
spring and early summer brought the assassinations of Martin Luther
King, Jr., and Robert F. Kennedy, and the closing weeks marked the
removal of Thomas Merton at the age of fifty-three, thus ending a life
that in the words of a recent biographer, "understood and revealed
much about the twentieth century and, in particular, the role of religion
within it."[2] For whatever twists and turns of attitude and belief Merton

may have shown, there was never a departure from the basic premise of religion and its enduring value in human lives.

To say that Merton's influence has been widespread and persistent, is to state the obvious. Few American writers of the second half of this century have had greater appeal for and influence on their contemporaries, and in Merton's case that has been especially true of intellectuals and of the young. It is notoriously difficult to analyze and weigh intellectual influence of any kind, and I shall not attempt it here. I wish merely to attest to the importance of Merton as a witness to what is increasingly recorded as the most important issue of the present hour, namely, the threat of nuclear warfare and all that this threat implies. This constitutes the 'heart of the matter' of this study, and though the evidence dates from a lengthy meditation about the tragedy of Hiroshima written in 1961, the intervening decades have produced nothing to lessen its significance; they have only served to heighten it. Moreover, it is David Givey's belief that Merton's position on nonviolence in the few years remaining to him after 1961 developed and matured. To be sure, his views incurred opposition, as they still do, and that from some of his own religious community at Gethsemani as well as from others outside the monastery. Yet he was not deterred on that account, for his sense of history made clear to him that a price has always to be paid for prophetic witness. As he told Jean Leclerq O.S.B., in a letter a few months before he died, "The vocation of the monk in the modern world, especially Marxist, is not survival but prophecy. We are all busy saving our skins."[3]

Did Thomas Merton see himself as a prophet? Perhaps. In any case, I think that when the history of American Catholicism since 1960 is written at a future date that will allow a reasonably long-range perspective, his name will figure prominently with people like Frank Sheed and Dorothy Day, to name only two of Merton's contemporaries who were prophets of our time, each in his and her own way. For prophecy does not consist solely in the ability to pierce the veil that hides the future and to predict its course; it partakes as well of the quality of a herald of God's message to humankind, a role that has been strikingly portrayed on a world scale by Mother Teresa of Calcutta and Helder Camara, Archbishop of Recife and Olinda.

While I do not pretend to know, I do wonder how much the writings of Merton on nonviolence and the mission of international peace may have influenced the thinking of the Catholic bishops of the United States during the last two decades. Of the fact of the bishops' notable change of view on war and peace, there is not the slightest doubt. One has only to think of their statements of 1966 and 1971 on the war in Vietnam to know what is meant. The qualified approval of that conflict in 1966 had by 1971 given way to a radical change to such a degree that they declared, "It is our firm conviction . . . that the speedy ending of this war is a moral imperative of the highest priority."[4] And the intervening decade has seen an even sharper turn from the traditional position of most Catholic bishops of this country.

It is in a context of this kind that Fr. Givey's book will prove helpful, for there is no likelihood that this question of public violence is going to receive a solution in the foreseeable future. On the contrary, there is every indication that the debate on the crucial issue of violence in general, and of nuclear warfare in particular, will deepen and spread in the time ahead. Pope John Paul II would seem to share this view in light of the theme he has chosen for the World Day of Peace, January 1, 1983, namely, "The Dialogue of Peace: A Challenge for Our Time." The present work can here make its best contribution as a careful analysis of the thought and writing on nonviolence of one of the most widely read American religious writers of the late twentieth century. Thomas Merton would probably be the first to acknowledge that he had not written the final word on this complicated subject, but he wrote a word that is worth reading and pondering as the 1980s move forward, and it is to that end that David Givey's book has rendered a signal service.

John Tracy Ellis
Professorial Lecturer in Church History
The Catholic University of America

Introduction

Very much a man of his own time, Thomas Merton is uniquely a man for our time. His work and message is as much a challenge today, if not more so, than in the 1960's when he embarked upon his critique of violence, war, racism and many aspects of American society.

Merton's warnings about the prospect of nuclear war, the spread of violence in society and the grave responsibility of American Catholics to work for peace echo forth today like a great clarion call to action. Merton gives us his way of nonviolence as means to achieve Christian goals in contemporary society. The way of nonviolence, as a way of life, and as a way of confronting society, becomes the way Merton offers to bring peace about and make it a reality.

I have tried in this book to present Merton the social commentator and essayist. The focus will be on Merton's love of the world and his criticism of it. The lesser known social dimensions of contemplation will be explored along with Merton's lifelong quest for unity. The main emphasis will be on Merton's Christian philosophy of nonviolence and all that it entails as a way of life.

This endeavor is a "beginning," it is not at all a complete theory or philosophy. Merton, himself never finished the formulation or expression of his thinking on nonviolence due to his tragic and untimely death in 1968. The challenge of Merton, however, continues to live on, and I have attempted here to synthesize and present that challenge along with the way of nonviolence as a blueprint for the mid-1980s. Where it goes from here, and what direction Christian nonviolence in the 1980s takes, is as much up to you, the reader, as it is to myself, the author. The bottom line of Merton's challenge is that if we believe in peace, then *we* must work for peace. If we want our society to be less violent then *we* must become nonviolent.

Thomas Merton was a truly human person, an authentically modern Christian. His questions are our questions, his doubts are our doubts, his fears are our fears. It is my hope in writing this book that his faith may also be ours, along with his courage, and his way of nonviolence. Unless we, like Merton, are radically committed to become peacemakers, than we do not deserve to be called Christians. His insights are grounded in the solid foundation of contemplation, his thoughts are enlightened by the Gospel message and sparked by the world around him. As we approach the second millenium, we too must be grounded in contemplation, founded upon the Gospels and at the same time be a vital part of the world events which make up the twentieth century.

Fifteen years ago nonviolence was a word which was not heard too frequently outside of certain select circles. When it was heard, it elicited looks of caution and dismay, and evoked responses that categorized it somewhere left of limbo. Ten years ago it was still spelled as a hyphenated word, "non-violence." It seemed to be more a negative concept of a half-baked idea. Certainly it was outside of mainstream Catholicism and not worthy of serious consideration by hierarch or ordinary. Today, Merton assuredly smiles from his vantage point atop the seven-storied mountain at the great journey made by his favorite concept. Having come full circle, and broken out of confining parameters to become a spiral, nonviolence today confronts the American Catholic Church and all peace-loving Christians as the way of hope and force of peace for the future. Not only is nonviolence today impressed upon our consciousness as one, strong and powerful word, but as a multifaceted concept, and indeed a way of life.

Merton has that unique timeless quality in his writing to tinge the conscience, move the heart and touch the person in the depths of their reality. We cannot read Merton and be content to leave his words as a merely sentimental or emotional experience. His words, if we really have ears to hear, must fire us up to greater commitment and action on behalf of peace. If his way of nonviolence is a valid alternative to war and conflict, and I believe that it is, and if peace is ever to be established in the world, and I believe that it can; then the beginnings of his ideas, presented here, must be taken up, refined, analyzed, developed, and constantly put before the hearts and minds of people everywhere. His words must be translated into action and brought to the lives and attention of the people who make the decisions for war and for peace. While our great country argues about the location and cost of a proposed Peace Academy, the challenge of Merton stands boldly as a great peace initiative.

Merton has been called "a man for all seasons," "a solitary explorer," "a man for our times"; Is he likewise a contemporary saint in the wings? Certainly he would laugh. He loved to laugh, especially at himself. His cause, however, has been introduced—the cause of peace. The first miracle has been duly noted, the American Catholic Church and its ordained leaders talking and writing about war, the arms race, and the way of nonviolence.

The next miracle is up to you and up to me—to live the way of nonviolence and work actively for peace.

David W. Givey
August 15, 1982
Merion Mercy Campus
Merion Station, Pennsylvania

Chapter I
The Evolution of Merton's Social Awareness

One of the most impressive characteristics of Thomas Merton is that he not only lived what he preached but that he personified in himself the ideals espoused in his writings.

Merton believed in being open, honest, and self-critical. He never hoped so much to be "right" as to ask the "right questions" no matter how painful or ambiguous the response might be. This attitude of openness and receptivity to new ideas and of willingness to change in the face of added dimensions is nowhere more evident than in Merton's own changing attitude toward the world and his relation to it.

It was the same young radical student at Columbia University in the late 1930s, who fled the world and entered the monastery in 1941, and maintained for over ten years that his responsibility toward his fellow man was purely spiritual, who finally emerged in the 1960s as one of America's most outspoken and influential commentators of current social events.

Between 1950 and 1960 Merton's emphasis moved distinctly from the other worldly to concerns of this world. His first years in the monastery were spent counseling Christians to leave the world to its own self-destruction and seek personal happiness in the security of a contemplative order.

In the late 1950s and throughout the 1960s, however, Merton encouraged Christians to work within their society for the betterment of all peoples and especially to establish peace. Merton became more and more involved with the social concerns of this world and felt himself to be an integral part of it, rather than an alien trapped within it.

As a young man educated in England and the United States, who traveled extensively in Europe, in Latin America, and the United States, Merton initially looked to the monastery for a sense of peace and as a way of shutting out the world.[1]

Although he later tried to repudiate this image, he described himself in his autobiography as the ". . . stereotype of the world-denying contemplative—the man who spurned New York, spat on Chicago, and tromped on Louisville, heading for the woods with Thoreau in one pocket, John of the Cross in another, and holding the Bible open at the Apocalypse."[2]

It was over a period of two decades that Merton's social awareness and concern for the world gradually emerged into full consciousness. In 1966 Merton was able to write, much to the surprise of many of his admirers: "I am . . . a man in the modern world. In fact, I *am* the world just as you are! Where am I going to look for the world first of all if not in myself?"[3]

Although Merton did not change his message about the evil of the world and the good monastic life, by the early 1950s his personal journals began to indicate that his attitude toward the world and the monastery was gradually changing. It was a slow, involved process of rethinking his basic presuppositions.

It took him ten years to reorganize his thoughts and re-evaluate his position on just what a monastic vocation involved. The seeds of social concern were beginning to germinate in the early 1950s and would eventually reach maturity and produce abundant fruit during the 1960s.

The early Merton was an "immobile nonentity" as he called himself; a product of psychological withdrawal, and it was time for a new Thomas Merton to emerge. "Coming to the monastery has been for me exactly the right kind of withdrawal. It has given me perspective. It has taught me how to live. And now I owe everyone else in the world a share in that life . . . my first human act is the recognition of how much I owe everybody else."[4]

Merton began to realize that the element of protest was essential to monasticism, that contemplation and social involvement were integral, and that each Christian had the responsibility and obligation to speak out.

This new perspective of turning again toward the world and involving himself in it and its problems eventually made Merton "one of the Church's most outspoken social critics . . . a thinker totally immersed in the problems of the world, a monk who was very much a man of the twentieth century."[5]

Authors have described Merton's change of attitude in varying ways, utilizing different terminology and theories. The descriptions range from "startling" and "dramatic" to "great" and "new."[6] Some authors see the tension which existed in Merton, between his love for solitude and his love for other people as an open contradiction,[7] rather than as a healthy dialectical tension compelling him forward and expanding his intellectual, spiritual, and personal horizons.

One commentator speaks of an "apparent contradiction" and opens the way to a real development within Merton. He states that Merton would often make some point, only later to assert what appeared to be diametrically opposed. The commentator goes on to say that this style of writing ". . . does not mean that [Merton's] thought has not been expressed in clear and concrete terms. It merely indicates that his thought is always fragmentary and always 'historical' in the sense that it was always centered upon that portion of reality which he was confronting even though it still retained, at least in his own mind, a definite relationship with what has gone before and what is yet to come. But because his own personality was so dynamic and so enthusiastic, he tended to give the impression that what he said in each case was an adequate expression of the matter at hand."[8]

At times there are inconsistencies and even contradictions in Merton's writings, but they reflect his developmental and dialectical approach to truth. Although Merton is not a systematic writer, he is more of an essayist, giving his opinion and impression of a particular issue as it confronted him. Merton used writing to learn and to teach. He would write to find out what the proper questions were that should be asked. He often wrote probingly and inquisitively looking for a response and perhaps rebuttal.

Ultimately Merton drew closer to other people and to their world, because he wrote about the problems and issues that confront modern people: alienation, violence, war, injustice, and the pursuit of peace and nonviolence. Merton wrote: "I feel myself involved in the same problems and I need to work out the problems of the world with other men because they are also my problems."[9]

Higgins is on target when he sees a cyclic development in Merton's thought,[10] as is McInerny who writes of a growing "awareness of a sense of responsibility toward society."[11]

In this developmental approach to Merton's attitude toward the world, much of the "gusto" Merton had for life as a young bon vivant and student is again directed outward to society. The major difference, however, is that Merton's vision of the world in the later part of his life has been refined by his monastic experience and filtered through his deep prayer life imbued and immersed in solitude.

Toward the end of his life Merton wrote: "We do not go into the desert to escape people but to learn how to find them; we do not leave them in order to have nothing more to do with them, but to find out the way to do them the most good."[12]

Naomi Burton, a long-time friend and editorial assistant to Merton wrote: "More and more it seems to me, the concerns of the last years of his life were the same concerns that occupied him in 1940. . . ."[13]

In a recent publication edited by Gerald Twomey, several of the writers who were old friends of Merton use this developmental approach in assessing Merton's stand on social issues toward the end of his life.[14] This is especially true regarding Merton's perspective on peacemaking, nonviolence, racial justice, and social concerns.[15]

Merton himself was aware of this development when in 1962 he wrote: ''Much that is spelled out in later books and articles is already implied in *The Seven Storey Mountain*. But it cannot really be seen until it is found in more articulate statements—or perhaps in more cryptic ones. . . .''[16]

Merton did not view these apparent contradictions in his life as negative elements. Instead, he saw his life as being ''almost totally paradoxical . . . [where the] very contradictions in my life are in some ways signs of God's mercy to me.''[17] Merton wrote about these paradoxical elements within himself as early as 1951 when he wrote in his journal, ''Like Jonas himself I find myself traveling toward my destiny in the belly of a paradox.''[18]

It is interesting and informative if we take Hegel's dialectical process and use it to analyze the development and progression of Merton's thought. Like all analyses and analogies, it is valid only so far; but it does give a key to the dynamic process taking place in Merton's social consciousness.

It can be said that Merton's thought followed the dialectical process of thesis, antithesis, and synthesis. This necessarily involved apparent contradictions and tensions. These contradictions are either resolved in greater truth, as Merton's reconciliation of contemplation and worldly involvement, or they are excluded as Merton's complete shutting out of the world.

Viewed in this way, it can be maintained that Merton's thought progressed in a dialogic process, forward and upward. It incorporated the most vital aspects and truths of each thesis-antithesis, always searching for a greater and greater synthesis of all the essential elements, especially that of contemplation and social concern. This process eventually culminated in an intellectual and social stance which was complementary rather than contradictory to his spiritual and contemplative orientation.

Merton's desire to live in genuine solitude and yet at the same time to assume more and more responsibility for the world was one of the greatest paradoxes in his life. More than a paradox, however, it is better described as a dialectic.

This dialectic was recognized in Merton by his Cistercian brother, John Eudes Bamberger, who, noting a tension between Merton's commitment to solitary contemplation and his concern for humanity, realized that open warfare never erupted (i.e., direct contradiction). This dialectic was kept in balance because of Merton's awareness of the two drives within him, which he realized were not mutually exclusive.[19]

This dialectical process was operative in Merton's fertile mind on several different planes. He had a special ability to synthesize the spiritual and the secular, the traditional and the transient, the eternal truths with the temporal presentation of these truths and contemplation with a world of action. He was, as one author stated: ". . . an Erasmian humanist who could speak universal truths in contemporary terms."[20]

Merton himself went through a dialectical process in the Hegelian sense in regard to his intellectual, spiritual, and social stance vis-à-vis the world. In this process the thesis is denied or negated by the antithesis; this negation is then negated or denied by the synthesis which embraces what is true in both the thesis and antithesis and brings us one step nearer to reality and truth.[21]

This dialectical process continues over and over, each time resulting in a new and further thesis, negated in turn and reconciled in a new synthesis. The term dialectic is thus used for "that process of conflict and reconciliation which goes on within reality itself, and within human thought about reality."[22]We could add, and within the thinking, developing person himself.

We can apply this dialectical analysis to Merton's life and thought, which are so intimately linked. The original thesis would be his total immersion in the secular world during the time of his education, culminating with his years at Columbia University. The antithesis, or opposite, would be his growing concern for social problems, especially the poor, and his desire to be a social worker in Harlem. This paradox or apparent contradiction was resolved by his conversion to Catholicism, his entrance into the monastery, and his renunciation of the world.

This synthesis in turn became a new thesis during the 1940s characterized by Merton's solitary life and almost total exclusion of the world and the affairs of men. The antithesis to this began to take shape in the early 1950s with contradictory tendencies of love for the world and men and concern for social problems. This was gradually resolved into a new synthesis in the mature Merton, who was the consummate contemplative, critical of social problems and advocating nonviolence and the pursuit of peace.

The new synthesis illustrated Merton's mature intellectual stance during the 1960s and was characterized by contemplation in a world of action. After more than thirty years of development, always open to new and different points of view, Merton reconciled the diverse and seemingly contradictory elements of his thought. He tried to live in almost total solitude, moving to a hermitage the last few months of his life, and yet was more involved than ever in the social problems of war, injustice, and racism. It was tragic indeed that Merton's untimely death brought this dialectical process to an abrupt end. Just at a time when Merton was opening up to the East and incorporating elements of Eastern mysticism into his synthesis, he died in Bangkok while on a journey to the East. This brought his journey of truth to an end.[23]

It is interesting to note that Bailey, a Protestant, writing about Merton's mysticism, and only tangentially touching on his social concerns, comes to the conclusion that Merton's "more mature works are almost entirely dialogic in nature. They are nearly devoid of finality and dogma. The principles enunciated are couched in heuristic form suggesting incomplete knowledge, a journey in process."[24]

Bailey's assessment is insightful when he says that a close reader of Merton is actually reading the interior dialectic of the author. Rather than the ambiguities and apparent contradictions being signs of inconsistency or intellectual vacillation, they are really manifestations of his "continuing synthesis."[25]

Throughout his life Merton continually posited a new antithesis, an opposite idea, for each synthesis or idea, not only in his own works but often in those of others. He was not a systematic writer and did not feel bound to produce irrefutable logic enshrined in perfect systems. The evolution of Merton's thought is really the unfolding of his life.

A significant element in this analysis of Merton's developing awareness is that he always chose to resolve a thesis-antithesis duality by the
application of Christian principles. This is one of the most significant
contributions that Merton has made to contemporary social commentary—his Christian perspective and the application of Christian principles to ethical and social problems.

Whether the issue was man's alienation, the evil of the city, war and
violence or racism, Merton always sought to apply the Gospel message
and Christian principles to the issue at hand. He especially tried to apply
the basic Christian principle of nonviolence to social questions as we
shall see later. Merton saw everything through the eyes of the contemplative, but more and more it was the eyes of the contemplative who
was vitally concerned with the social problems of society.

Merton's unique perspective was, of course, both a limitation and a
strength. It seems, however, that the strengths far surpass the limitations. His view was limited because the monastic life is not the totality
of the Church or of society.

It is a strength, on the other hand, because it afforded Merton the
open space needed for real evaluation and the distance necessary for
true criticism. The monastic life also allowed him to be a man of single
purpose, a lone warrior, and solitary explorer. The perspective from the
monastery window was one of objectivity and insightful vision.

Rather than being embroiled in the day-to-day issues of life and its
exigencies, Merton was able to retain his own solidarity and unique-
ness. After quiet and mature reflection filtered through his own experience, he was able to comment on the most trying and vexing issues
facing the human family. This gave him a voice which no journalist,
editorialist, political analyst, or bishop could claim. It made what he
said and wrote valuable because of its depth, worthwhile because of its
perspective, and significant because of its spiritual vision and Christian
scope.

We are still confronted with the obvious question: Why? Why this
change in attitude and emphasis on the part of Merton. What accounted

for the development which took place in his thought and writing which eventually lead to his contemporary Christian social ethic and philosophy of nonviolence?

These are crucial questions because his writings are so reflective of Merton the man. Merton was always an intuitive and creative writer. He treated issues and situations as they struck him, and he reflected and commented on them aloud through his writing. The formative factors of his own intellectual and personal development are keys in understanding much of what he wrote. Merton the man and monk can never be divorced from Merton the writer, poet, thinker, or social commentator.

When *The Sign of Jonas* appeared in 1953, it was difficult to predict what direction Merton's writings might take in the future. Observers did notice a significant modification of some of Merton's earlier views. One reviewer in the *New Republic* magazine pointed out the decisive change in Merton's outlook. This reviewer made a very good comparison of Merton's experience to the experience of the man in Plato's allegory of the cave. The man is freed from his chains, rushes out into the sunlight, and though blinded for some time by the brightness, eventually recovers his sight, learns about the real world, and returns to the cave to help his fellow men slip out of their chains.[26]

In this comparison Merton rushed out of the shadowy world of New York City into the "real world" of light, the monastery, and his early writings revealed a man who was still blinded by the glorious light. *The Sign of Jonas*, however, showed how well his eyes were adjusting and how he had come to feel the inevitable desire to return to the world in order to help those still in their chains.[27]

The appearance of *The Seeds of Destruction* in 1964 had proven to everyone that Merton was thoroughly immersed in the world's problems. This was followed by Merton's books and articles on nonviolence, violence in society, war, and racism. It was obvious that he had reached a new state of development.

There are innumerable factors which contributed to the formation and evolution of Merton's social consciousness. We shall consider some of the salient and most consistent of these factors. Of primary importance as a contributing factor was Merton's vision of the role of a monk and his re-evaluation of the monk's place in the Church and modern world.

During his conversion stage, Merton had been convinced that the most moral stance he could take vis-à-vis modern society was simply to live fully and totally as a monk—a life which was a contradiction to everything that society held dear. He gradually came to see, however, that passive protest of that kind was no longer enough. Unless one spoke out and acted against the evil of society he may, by silent complicity share the guilt for these evils.[28]

More and more Merton came to the realization that ". . . when speech is in danger of perishing or being perverted in the amplified noise of beasts, perhaps it becomes obligatory for a monk to try to speak."[29]

Merton maintained that one of the essential tasks of the monk was to fulfill his "prophetic" function. The monk's prophetic function was not as concerned with seeing into the future as seeing into the present. He said that "To prophesy is not to predict, but to seize upon reality in its moment of highest expectation and tension toward the new. This tension is discovered not in hypnotic elation but in the light of everyday experience."[30]

As a contemplative, Merton had a real insight into contemporary times and the deepest troubles that confronted men and women. He felt that part of the role of the monk as prophet, like that of the poet or artist, was to be aware of immature and inadequate expressions of ideas that are given currency and refuse to be dominated or influenced by them.

Merton felt that poets, artists, and prophets have greater freedom and should use it for deeper insights and expressions of the reality of man's human condition. "Unfortunately," he complained in 1966, "the confusion of our world has made the message of our poets obscure and our prophets seem to be altogether silent."[31]

To live as a monk is to live in constant protest against the evils of society and the world. Thomas Merton always considered the protest to be an integral part of the monastic vocation. Initially, he thought his leaving the world for the monastery would be protest enough, but soon realized that he was compelled to speak out in protest against the most blatant evils in society.

In order to accomplish this, the monk must discover himself so that he can give himself totally to God and gain the insight and vision necessary to be a prophet and critic of society. Merton believed that modern society with its emphasis on mass-man, mass-media, and conformism was itself one of the greatest obstacles to man's discovering his true identity. Merton thus felt compelled to protest all that in society stifled man's spontaneity, his search for self and God.

Merton's life in the monastery led him to the realization of the social implications of solitude and the contemplative. As he was fond of saying, the true solitary goes into the desert ". . . not to escape other men but in order to find them in God."[32]

A second important factor in understanding Merton's evolving attitude toward the world was his critical view of himself. He possessed a great ability to examine his own conscience, to criticize himself and be open to other opinions and points of view. This explains to a large degree Merton's ability to move from one emphasis to another and to be flexible and creative in his thinking and writing.

Merton was his own worst critic and thought that he had written too much. He once described himself, with characteristic humor, as "the author of more books than necessary."[33]

Questions were important for Merton, and he was forever asking them of himself and others. He felt that a person is known better by the questions that he asks than by any answers he might give. He was a self-questioning person and a true thinker which meant that he was constantly going over what he had written and looking at it from another perspective or point of view—again the dialectical approach to truth. He was continually reviewing his thoughts and testing them for stability and durability.[34]

A third factor in Merton's social development was his sense of history and the conviction that he and all Christians must take some responsibility for the world. Merton felt that since God was working in history no one could be a true contemplative or a Christian without a sense of history and of historical responsibility.

Although not all commentators agree that Merton had a realistic sense of history he demonstrated time and time again that he felt a responsibility to help direct the course of events in time. Bailey has a valid point when he states that for Merton the contemplative discovers himself within the dialectical movement of history and enters into conscious dialogue with history.[35]

As he became increasingly convinced that the atmosphere in the United States during the 1960s was in many respects like that in Germany in the 1930s, Merton sought to remind Americans and especially Christians of their responsibilities. He was upset with the indifference of so many American intellectuals in the face of tendencies toward political totalism. Merton acquired a deep appreciation for men like Dietrich Bonhoeffer, Alfred Delp, Franz Jägerstätter, and Max Metzer, who had the courage to stand up against the evils of their day, when virtually their whole society opposed them.[36]

Addressing one of his most sarcastic letters to American intellectuals, Merton called upon them not to stand "innocently by" as social evils were perpetuated in society.[37] He forcefully stated that intellectuals cannot be "bystanders," for their waiting is harmful and an only excuse for inaction.

He consistently referred to the intellectuals as "we" who have the responsibility to resist the evils forced on society by "they," the "powerful ones" who rule and seek power over all "the others," the great majority. He considered this a personal challenge as much as a challenge issued to others.

If the intellectuals do nothing, then they must face the ultimate challenging question: "Do we have any choice left? Worse still: are we not the kind of bystanders whose very 'innocence' makes them guilty, makes them the obvious target for arbitrary terror?"[38]

A fourth factor in Merton's move from spiritual to social writer was his deep desire to be a saint and strive for sanctity. He was convinced that anyone who really wanted to become a saint, if he really put himself to the task, could be one. Some of Merton's earliest books were about the lives of the saints and potential saints and they afforded him great insight into the characters of those who were truly holy.[39]

A common characteristic Merton discovered among saints was their compassion for other human beings. The saints were real people whose primary saintly quality was their deep concern for the needs of others. Before a person could become a saint, Merton concluded, he or she must first become a person, "in all the humanity and fragility of man's actual condition."[40]

Just as Merton recognized the element of compassion in the lives of the saints, Twomey sees compassion as the key to the evolution of Merton's own social consciousness. He sees compassion as being the "wellspring of Merton's social concern" and as the quality which gives him insight into the social and political problems of society.[41]

For Merton sanctity was not a matter of being less human, but more human than other people. This implied a greater capacity for concern, for suffering and understanding, and also for humor and joy and for appreciation of the good and beautiful things of life.[42]

Another dimension of Merton's opening out to the world was the realization that sanctity consisted in a person truly being himself. Rather than stressing the strong self-abnegation of which he wrote earlier he now stated: "For me to be a saint means to be myself. Therefore, the problem of sanctity and salvation is in fact the problem of finding out who I am and of discovering my true self."[43]

This quest for the true self became one of Merton's lifelong searches. This search for personal identity was a very important factor in the social dimension of contemplation which we will discuss later. This theme likewise reflects the basis of the search for peace which occupied much of Merton's later writing: ". . . there is only one problem on which all my existence, my peace and my happiness depend: to discover myself in discovering God. If I find Him I will find myself and if I find my true self I will find Him."[44]

A fifth causative factor in Merton's social development was the re-newal of monasticism which gave him a greater knowledge of world affairs, through greater access to sources of information. The first ten years of his monastic life were lived under very strict rules. The liberalization of the Trappist order in general and of Gethsemani Abbey in particular during the late 1940s and early 1950s was very instrumental in the early change in Merton.

By the 1960s Merton was writing that he had come in contact with other solitudes, with the loneliness, the simplicity, the perplexity of novices and scholastics of his own monastic community, and with the loneliness of people everywhere, even of those outside the Church.

He considered the majority of the mass media to be a source of grave confusion to the contemplative, and relied instead upon a highly selective source of books and quality journals and periodicals. His normal procedure in commenting on any given issue was to wait for several months for the topic to crystallize. He would then have a greater objectivity and perspective.

A sixth element that was intrumental in changing Merton's attitude toward the world was his opportunity to meet the world again after many years of monastic seclusion. He realized that after many years he could love the world that he had once seemed to hate and reject. His journeys into nearby Louisville served to re-inforce his growing love of and involvement with other people.

In what seemed to be almost a mystical experience, he wrote about a journey into Louisville, in 1957: "Thank God, thank God that I *am* like other men, that I am only a man among others. . . . It is a glorious destiny to be a member of the human race, though it is a race dedicated to many absurdities and one which makes many terrible mistakes. . . . I have the immense joy of being a man, a member of a race in which God Himself became incarnate."[45]

A decisive event took place on June 22, 1951, during one of Merton's trips into Louisville, an event which provides a seventh factor in his change of attitude. On that day Merton visited the Federal District Court and became a citizen of the United States.

Merton had written in his journal *The Sign of Jonas* that he had not really possessed a nationality for the first thirty-six years of his life and had always been proud of his freedom. As a naturalized citizen of the United States, however, he began to feel more like a citizen of the Kingdom of God begun on earth.

In his book on Merton, the social critic, Baker feels that much of what Merton wrote in the mid-1950s on war, the bomb, racial conflict, and nonviolence may well have had their origin in his oath of allegiance to the United States. "For as an American citizen," Baker said about Merton, "he came to feel more and more responsible for his country's salvation and perfection."[46]

An eighth and final factor of unusual significance upon Merton's view of the world was undoubtedly that of Pope John XXIII. Merton derived many of his principles of nonviolence and social justice from Pope John and especially his encyclical *Pacem in Terris (Peace on Earth.*

Merton was so impressed by this social encyclical which appeared in 1963 that he wrote an "official" interpretation and response to it and incorporated its key concepts into his future social commentaries.[47]

One aspect of Pope John's writings that Merton greatly agreed with was the Pope's intent to preserve the independent authority of the small and struggling nations. Merton was especially fond of quoting Pope John's words warning more powerful nations not to unjustly oppress struggling nations or to unduly meddle in their affairs.

Merton was influenced by Pope John's view of authority which should be based on moral force and love and not physical force or military strength. He was likewise encouraged by the good Pope's optimistic view of man and the world.

These were two men who believed in people. Merton was quick to realize that Pope John was open to all people and to the world, and he was honest enough to ask himself, "Am I?" The power for peace in the great encyclical of Pope John, *Peace on Earth,* was based on its profound and optimistic Christian spirit which embraced all peoples in every corner of the world. This perspective enriched and enlarged Merton's vision and served to strengthen and quicken the evolution of his own social consciousness so that it too could embrace the world and all its problems.

The World and Its Problems

With the publication of his *Disputed Questions* in 1960, Merton began to discuss some specific social questions. He admitted that some of the topics were more or less controversial. That did not mean, however, that he was engaging in controversy with anyone in particular. He was, on the contrary, ". . . simply thinking out loud about certain events and ideas which seem to me to be significant, in one way or another, for the spiritual and intellectual life of modern man."[48]

A basic theme which runs throughout this book is that of the relation of the person to the social organization. Merton went so far as to maintain that the problem of the person and the social organization was one of the most important, if not the most important problem of our century. "Every ethical problem." he wrote, "of our day—especially the problem of war—is to be traced back to this root question."[49]

In this book Merton treated many of the topics which were to occupy his writings for the next eight years; the problem of individualism as opposed to personalism, the need for solitude and true humanism, the illusions of modern society, and the final integration of the mature person.

The first chapter of *Disputed Questions,* entitled "The Pasternak Affair" capsulized, in many ways the direction that Merton's social thought would follow. This chapter included many points of his later critique and put forward Merton's ideals of a mature, contemporary Christian.

Merton wrote this chapter on the occasion of the death of Boris Pasternak—May 30, 1960, the renowed Russian poet and author who refused the Noble Prize for Literature in 1958 for his novel *Dr. Zhivago,* because of the pressure from the Soviet Government. Many of the qualities for which Merton praised Pasternak were equally applicable to himself.

These words written by Merton about Pasternak can easily be applied to Merton ". . . he was a man who stands first of all for the great spiritual values that are under attack in our materialistic world."[50] Likewise, Merton writes that the Russian poet is the symbol of the highest spiritual and human values, and that his existential dedication was to the supreme inner value of personalism which is one of the characteristic Christian contributions to Western humanistic thought.

Merton sought to do as Pasternak did: ". . . to speak my mind out of love for man, the image of God—not to speak a set piece dictated by my social situation."[51] Both men wanted to assess the significance of social and political events for the spiritual and intellectual life of their times.

Again, Merton's description of Pasternak mirrors his own perspective: "Both as a writer and as a man, Pasternak stands out as a sign of contradiction in our age of materialism, collectivism and power politics. His spiritual genius is essentially and powerfully solitary . . . his significance . . . lies in the fact that his very solitude made him capable of extraordinarily intimate and understanding contacts with men all over the face of the earth."[52]

Pasternak's protest was, in reality, a protest of life itself, of humanity itself. The protest contained in his writings, as in Merton's own writings during the 1960s, awakened the guilt of a society that had consciously and knowingly betrayed life and sold itself out to falsity, formalism and spiritual degradation.

Merton applauded Pasternak, and later followed his example, for taking up his pen and giving spiritual and moral resistance to the political forces of society, for advocating a deep, inner freedom for all people and for having a vision which saw all peoples as the image of God. Both writers attempted to defend a liberty of the spirit which Merton felt was as threatened with death in the West as it was behind the Iron Curtain.

Merton's optimism found a kindred spirit in Pasternak who believed that there was an exit, a solution of man's social problems and ills. The solution which could bring meaning out of evil and peace out of war and violence was love—the highest expression of man's spirituality and freedom.

In commenting on Pasternak, Merton gave an insight into his own view of history and the challenge that it contained for Christians: "History is not a matter of inexorable scientific laws, it is a new creation, a work of God in and through man . . . history (however) has never yet really had a chance to become a Christian creation. For the world to be changed, man himself must begin to change it, he must take the initiative, he must step forth and make a new kind of history. The change begins within himself."[53]

As Merton's social writings became more pointed he often reminded Christians of their responsibilities and tasks. He maintained that the Christian is bound to build a just, humane and peaceful society on earth. The ethical and social implications of saving one's soul mean that man must live a human life in the best and fullest sense. Merton delineated the presuppositions of this Chirstian humanism: ". . . a reasonable standard of living, a certain freedom, opportunities for education, decent work, and mature participation in the political and cultural life of society. In a word, Christian living supposes a balanced and peaceful social order."[54]

Certain movements and characteristics of society were seen by Merton as extremely detrimental to the establishment and flowering of this Christian vision of society. One of these which fell under Merton's verbal attack was that of mass-man. He describes mass-man as: ". . . the passive, inert man who drifts with the crowd and never decides anything for himself."[55] Masses may be called, he once wrote, but only persons are chosen.

Mass society was also a concern for Merton, and all that it inevitably led to, like alienation. He used the term alienation in reference to a human being who is systematically kept, or who, for any reason, allows himself to be kept, in a social situation in which he exists purely and simply for somebody else. Mass society abets the alienation process precisely because it tends to keep man from fully achieving his identity or developing his potential. The dimension of overcontrol especially contributes to the frustration and alienation experienced by so many contemporary people. Merton is very critical of the elements of over-control in our affluent, consumer American society. Advertising in particular treats the consumer consistently as a minor and maintains him in a state of psychological passivity and dependence.

The great temptation for many people is escape from the pressures of mass society by getting lost in the great formless sea of irresponsibility and anonymity of the crowd. There is however, no more dangerous solitude than that of the man who is lost in the crowd.[56]

The true solitary, on the other hand, is often the one with the most to say, not because he uses many words but what he says is new, substantial and unique. It is his own, seen from his own unique perspective. A solitary has something vital to say because he is a real and authentic person himself. Merton, as Pasternak too, were solitary explorers in a world of lonely people, and for that reason they stood out as guides and leaders challenging our conscience and lighting our way.

Merton issued numerous warnings to the type of person who "adjusted" to society and its demands but was really, in existential terms, alienated and estranged to himself. This type of person lives in a world which is cluttered with his possessions, his projects, his exploitations, his machinery, but is not able to get in touch with his real self. It seems to be the nature of modern society to promote and perpetuate this alienation. Frequently persons are caught in this paradox of appearing to be a "success" in society, but in reality they are being consumed by it. He is then no longer capable of experiencing the truth that he is himself rooted and grounded in God's love.

This person, consequently, is full of inner divisions because he is kept from unifying himself by a society which pulls and tugs in a hundred different directions. It was precisely for this kind of person that Merton advocated contemplation and solitude, at least in small doses, to enable the individual to get in touch with his own reality, and to heal the divisions within himself.

The mass media serve to reinforce this alienation within society and within individuals by reducing so much that is vital to sweeping generalities, terse documentaries, and sensational specials. Merton called the mass media a tepid medium which reduced to formless neutrality and "news" the realities of Christianity, in order to gain nothing more than "publicity."

Like his approach to politicians in general, Merton's attitude toward the mass media was one of his few, but persistent, prejudicies. The mass media represented for him one of the more sinister forces operating within American culture. As was often the case, Merton made sweeping, indiscriminate judgments, frequently simplistic, but usually with some acute and perceptive observations.

He envisioned the mass media acting, albeit unconsciously, in conspiratorial conjunction with the politicians, militarists, and financiers who were attempting to exploit the masses. He felt they promulgated information to the public in such a manner that, while disseminating the "party line," they put the people under the illusion that they were thinking things out for themselves. This is due, "to the isolation of the individual in mass society, in which he is in fact a zero in the crowd in which he is absorbed."[57]

The mass media was just one social problem that fell under Merton's critical knife. During the 1960s Merton wrote more than twenty books, half of these were devoted, at least to some degree, to social topics. Between 1963 and his untimely death in 1968 he wrote his most outspoken books and articles on the subjects of war and race which he considered the two major social problems confronting modern society.

The underlying thesis of these books was that modern society was in an advanced state of moral decay. This was attributable to the fact that man had become almost completely despiritualized. In other words, contemporary man had lost his sense of the Divine, the importance of the transcendent, and concern for the eternal realities and how they affect the here and now. This state of affairs, in turn, has been precipitated by modern man's mindless commitment to materialism and consumerism.

Merton's writings took on a sense of urgency. He cried out to the Catholic intellectual: "Our duty to preserve the human person in his integrity, his freedom and his individuality, and to arm him spiritually against the peril of totalitarianism is not just something it would be nice for us to discuss and perhaps to study. It is an urgent task which demands insistently to be carried out. . . . It is the most important task of the Catholic intellectual. . . ."[58]

Merton advocated a socially oriented contemplation as a response to this urgent task and calling. This form of contemplative prayer and approach to Christianity would enable the person to discover God through discovering his real identity, always in communion with other people. This philosophy of union through active contemplation necessitated, at the same time, an involvement in and change of social structures, especially unjust ones, and the fabric of society itself.

Social Change

Thomas Merton was never a person to do anything halfway, or halfheartedly. Once he set upon a course of action or a task, whether it be praying, writing, or thinking, he did it with full enthusiasm and determination. It was no wonder then, that once he made the transition to a more socially oriented approach to spirituality and writing he would advocate social change of the most fundamental nature, both in structure and attitude.

He maintained that Christian social action was first of all action which discovers religion in work, in politics and in social programs, not only, or so much to win workers for Christ, but because every man is our brother. His social ethic saw Christianity in all of social life, as ". . . liberating man from misery, squalor, sub-human living conditions, economic or political slavery, ignorance and alienation . . . Christian social action must liberate man from all forms of servitude, whether economical, political or psychological."[59]

Kelly succinctly summarizes Merton's notion of social action as implying three major emphases: first, emphasis on the human as distinct from the merely collective or technological, and affirmation of man as opposed to production processes; second, emphasis on the personal, and personal values. These are essentially spiritual and incommunicable, promoting respect for man's right to be himself, to think for himself, his right to freedom, friendship, creativity, and love. Third, emphasis on a sapiential viewpoint that enables man to see life in its wholeness, with stability and purpose.[60]

All Christians should be socially concerned and should view social ideals and programs in the light of the word of God. The norm of acceptance or rejection of any program should be the measure of authentic respect and love it manifests for the human person. In this way nonviolence as a way of life can become more realizable in society as a Christian and human mode of existence for the modern Christian.

Merton's social teaching began to take shape as he developed his thought in his writings. He sought to attune people to the awareness of Christ in the world today as a basic intuition upon which society and all creation must be renewed. The task for the Christian is to seek and find Christ in the modern world as it is, not as it might be. In this Merton was a realist, but he knew it would be difficult and at times frustrating. He encouraged Christians, especially the American Christians to choose the world as a task and vocation, more concerned with transforming the world into a new creation of Jesus Christ than with amassing large sums of money, land or profits.

The evolution of Merton's social awareness took all the best elements of his contemplative spirituality and joined them with the social dimension of life in the world. In order to achieve this blend of the sacred and the secular a person must have, like Merton himself, a world view that envisions man and his world, and Christ and the world as interpenetrating. Such a Christic world view is dynamic and alive. It involves decision and commitment. Merton exhorted Christians to develop a personal world view modeled on St. Paul's vision of all creation "groaning and travailing in pain" (Rom. 8:22) in the continuing act of evolving creation.

Merton opposed a static model of a sacred and hierarchical cosmos in which all things are decided beforehand and where the only choice is to accept that which is imposed as part of an immobile and established social structure. He was against a static dualism in life or world view and encouraged a deep tolerance and understanding for change, diversity, and development. Again, his openness was a major factor in this attitudinal development, and was to expand as he grew in the breadth of his vision.

Understanding this world view it is easier to comprehend Merton's concept of social change. Man's physical world is changing due to technological innovation and the emergence of new philosophies of social organization and development. With the consequent altering of sociological structures, man's social world is also changing. Merton's position was that the Christian today must help direct and control the forces of change in the modern world. The Christian cannot let the directional force of society depend on someone else, some other ideology, or chance.

Christians have the obligation to enhance and promote true human freedom, fight to eradicate injustices in society and develop man's capacity for love. This is especially true in the promotion of peace and nonviolence which means attacking the problems of war and racism head-on. The greatest threat in accomplishing this task is what Merton labeled "moral passivity . . . the most terrible danger of our time."[61]

As we saw before Merton was influenced in this type of thinking by Pope John XXIII and the Second Vatican Council. The Council called for Christians to take a more active and positive role in their society, and its transformation. Vatican II stated: "Christ taught us that the new command of love was the basic law of human perfection and hence of the world's transformation."[62]

Merton became a voice of conscience uttering the prophetic plea, not just for social reform, but for the transformation of a whole culture and society and of their materialistic values. He recognized and often pointed out the "seeds of destruction" in the reformers as well as in the "establishment."

His role became that of prophet, as he himself defined it: "One who has been struck by the word of God. The word of God has entered his life and disrupted it and, through his life, disrupts the lives of other."[63]

Liberal utopianism has failed to give confidence in inevitable progress; false optimism is as useless as misguided patriotism is dangerous. The Christian must commit himself to an eschatology of hope: ". . . for eschatology is not *finis* and punishment, the winding up of accounts and the closing of books: it is the final beginning, the definitive birth into a new creation. It is not the last gasp of exhausted possibilities but the first taste of all that is beyond conceiving as actual."[64]

Thus Merton's call for social change was not based on economic or materialistic exigencies, nor solely upon humanistic concerns. His was a specifically Christian call for social change, based on Christian principles of action with an eschatological thrust based on hope. Christians should transcend earthly political boundaries and strive for a transcultural integration.[65] This is in harmony with Merton's basic teaching on contemplation, union, and nonviolence, in which the individual, by discovering and becoming himself fully, at the same time transcends himself.

This understanding of the Christian-in-the-world led one writer to describe Merton as a "contemplative at the heart of the world, a world of revolution."[66] The practical ethical implications of this approach, of course, are manifold and complex and often controversial.

Each person's contribution must at least be the assertion of his or her own integrity and personality. Christian social endeavor is not so much a question of "doing something," although Merton certainly encouraged action. It is primarily concerned with "being someone." Otherwise mindless and misguided action, jumping on the latest bandwagons and frenzied activity will merely be an illusion and escape. The Christian must endeavor to change the social structures of his world through nonviolence, collaboration, communication, dialogue, and personal conversion. It involes nothing less than the total, whole person.

This can only be accomplished by an inner transformation of the individual person, who will in turn change society. The Christian must proceed by means of love, insight, and persuasion, through dialogue and mutual understanding, to collaborate with others in transforming the world into the kingdom of God. Contemplation and solitude are essential for a person to come into contact with his inner true self, to establish authentic communion with other people and to be in harmony with God.

How modern man is to achieve this inner transformation, reach true identity, and acquire a spirit of nonviolence is a key issue if he is to effect social change. Thus we will now consider the social dimensions and implications of contemplation as the basis for union and nonviolence.

Chapter II
The Social Dimensions of Contemplation

We have traced the development of Thomas Merton's attitude toward the world which gradually evolved over a period of twenty years into that of a mature monk who was able to combine contemplative silence with concern for the problems of society.

As his concern for the ills of the world sharpened its focus his need for contemplation deepened its penetration. Merton became increasingly convinced of the need of some contemplation for all people of good will. The early Merton advocated that sincere Christians flee the world and enter the solitude of the monastery. The mature Merton, on the other hand, encouraged all people to engage in contemplative prayer yet remain in the midst of the world of action. His views of contemplation took on social dimensions and became all-encompassing. He developed what might be called a philosophy of contemplation and union which formed the indispensable basis for his Christian philosophy of nonviolence.

We can say that Merton's philosophy of contemplation *is* his philosophy of union, for they are really different dimensions of the same dynamic. "Contemplation," he wrote, "is the highest expression of man's intellectual and spiritual life. It is life itself, fully awake, fully active, fully aware. . . ."[1] The aim of contemplation is union; greater and greater unity with self, other people and God. Reality should be sought in unity, not in division. People who live in disunity and division, on whatever level, are alienated, separated, and living in death. It is this division which is the root source of violence within individuals which eventually erupts into violence in society. Thus union heals the wounds of division, the source of inner violence, and leads to a non-violent spirit. Unity is necessary if nonviolence is ever to become a reality.

People seek unity in order to fulfill themselves, to gain possession of their lives, to "get themselves together," as we would say today. Solitude is essential to accomplish this difficult task. And solitude is very difficult to find in contemporary society.

Merton advocated contemplative solitude as the way by which we can discover ourselves; as the experience of finding meaning in life, of providing a basis for order in life, which in turn makes authentic life possible.

His concept is extremely existential and personalistic. A person is fully alive only when he experiences, at least to some extent, that he is spontaneously dedicating himself to the real purpose of his own personal existence. "Man is truly alive when he is aware of himself as the master of his own destiny to life or to death. . . . Man 'finds himself' when he is able to be aware that his freedom is spontaneously and vigorously functioning to orientate his whole being toward the purpose it craves . . . life in the fullest sense of the word."[2]

Seen even deeper, contemplation is the existential appreciation of one's own "nothingness" and apartness. This existential experience of "nothingness" is not a bottomless vortex of "no exit." Merton envisioned it, rather, as an abyss opening up in the center of one's deepest being. This abyss of interior solitude is a hunger which seeks more and more reality and greater and greater union with all being.[3]

This concept of contemplation is thoroughly Christian, for this hunger, originating in the center of our being will never be satisfied with any created thing, but yearns for union with Christ.

From this perspective, contemplation actually leads a person to the fulfillment of his being. "Contemplation is the sudden intuitive penetration of what really IS. It is the unexpected leap of the spirit of man into the existential luminosity of Reality Itself, not merely by the metaphysical intuition of being, but by the transcendent fulfillment of an existential communion with Him Who Is.''[4]

Merton's presentation of contemplation is both profoundly human and deeply Christian. The emphasis is on contemplation leading to the highest form of self-realization. In this process a person throws off his false self and discovers his real self. Division is healed as the real self is united with the inner-most depths of one's being.

The person commonly identified as ''I,'' is, in reality, our empirical self—the facade we portray to others, the image we try to emulate, the person we want to be. Through the solitude of contemplation, however, there emerges, if we are honest and persevering enough, the transcendent self that manifests itself deep inside our very being. This real self is in opposition to the superficial, external self, designated so casually with the pronoun ''I.''

Modern society glutted with advertisements, mass media, billboards, and ''junk'' mail is constantly telling people what they should wear, drink, eat, and drive. We are advised how we should live, how we should dress, and why we need more of almost everything—if not more, at least a bigger and better edition. Contemplation enables us to come to the awareness that the ''I'' created by and manipulated by society is really ''not I'' at all, but an image, a fabrication, an illusion, and a mask.

Too often the ''I'' that works in the world, which is able to survive, and is successful, is really nothing but a vesture and disguise of that mysterious and too often unknown ''self.'' The real self many of us never discover until we are dead.[5]

Merton's philosophy is radically human because he urges people to be themselves. It is essentially Christian because a person discovers himself in discovering God in Christ, and Christ within himself. We are each charged with the task of cooperating with God in the creation of our own lives, identities, and destinies. We are each called to share with God the work of creating the truth of our identity. We must rid ourselves of the false self, and all that goes along with it: division, hatred, fear, war, violence, materialism, and sin. We must do this in unity with other people for "we must look for (our) identity, somehow, not only in God but in other men."[6]

Anyone who wishes to be freed from his false self must be freed by the ground of being, the God whom he meets in contemplation. Merton described this freedom as birth, spiritual birth, which frees a person from the womb of society. He admitted that there is a time for each person to be comfortable and warm in the social womb, or the collective myth. There is, however, a time to be born, for "he who is spiritually 'born' as a mature identity is liberated from the enclosing womb of myth and prejudice."[7]

Seeking contemplation—a little time and open space to get in touch with ourselves and our God—is not then, an escape from time and matter or from social responsibility. It is rather a journey into the desert of one's own soul to discover there the meaning and mystery of life, thus enabling one to be himself and feel a oneness with all others. This is the social dimension of contemplation. The social function is precisely to enable the contemplative, whether he lives in a monastery or Philadelphia, to realize values and realities with a clarity which is impossible for someone totally immersed in worldly cares and concerns.

Merton wrote: "My solitude is not my own, for I see how much it belongs to them (others)—and that I have a responsibility for it in their regard, not just in my own. It is because I am one with them—there are no strangers."[8]

Early in his life as a monk Merton listed three kinds of contemplation following the traditional breakdown. All three were legitimate, and each recognized man's basic differences and vocations.

The first, natural contemplation, is the contemplation of "the artist, the philosopher and of the most advanced pagan religions." The second, active contemplation, is that of the baptized Christian who lives in society and uses the Church's aids—the sacraments, the liturgy, penance, prayer, meditation, and spiritual reading—to keep him close to God. The third, infused, passive or mystical contemplation, is the contemplation of the monk in which full time is given to meditation and to the Church's aids and in which the monk devotes his entire being to a search for the beatific vision.[9]

Ten years later, in one of his last books, Merton described contemplation in much broader terms, giving four points of agreement between the great contemplative traditions of the East and West. Although they sometimes differ quite radically in the formulation of aims and methods, Eastern and Western contemplatives agree substantially that by spiritual disciplines a person can change his life and find deeper meaning, integration, and fulfillment. There is agreement that there is more to human life than simply "getting somewhere" in politics, business, or even the Church; that man's highest ambition lies beyond "ambition," in the renunciation of the self; and finally that the purification of the will and intelligence can lead one to a deeper understanding of the meaning of life and of the very nature of Being itself.[10]

According to Merton, every person, regardless of his station in life, needs these elements of contemplation to make his life meaningful and to motivate him to aim for proper goals. Without some contemplation, some solitude, man falls prey to the depersonalization of modern society, to the myriad distractions, illusions and glittering gems offered from all sides.

How many times have we felt that we simply cannot "cope" that we cannot "get it together," that we were coming apart at the seams. Merton addressed people who have felt this way, and directed them to set aside some quiet time alone. His advice was simply to get in communion with themselves and with their God—experience contemplation and unity, experience peace and nonviolence—in other words, live.

Merton frequently insisted that a person could have inner peace and experience contemplation even in the heart of downtown Manhattan. It would not be easy, he realized that, but it could be done if a person was willing to pay the price of going against many of the accepted norms of society.

Basically there are two requirements necessary to follow in order to acquire the contemplative spirit in the midst of an urban center. First, a person must try, as far as possible, to reduce the conflict and frustration in his life by cutting down some of the superfluous contacts with the world and its distractions. This means reducing the need for pleasure, comfort, recreation, prestige, and success, and embracing a life of true spiritual poverty and detachment.

Second, a person must strive to put up with the inevitable conflicts that remain—the noise, the agitation, the crowds, lack of time. Above all he must try to overcome the constant contact with a purely secular mentality which is around us everywhere and at all times.[11]

This approach helps to simplify our lives, free us of some of the clutter which is constantly thrown our way. The experience of solitude also helps us to appreciate our fellow man on a deeper level. This kind of healthy and positive solitude enables us to discover ourselves and to discover other people in ourselves. When we find other people this way and begin to appreciate them anew, we realize that they are made in the image of God.

Thus, rather than being a "flight from the world" seeking contemplative solitude is really a movement of liberation and discovery. It is the acquisition of a new and higher perspective. It is a perspective free of the chaos and absurdity of our everyday world. It is based on the belief that God lives within us and that we are one with him and others when we are one with ourselves.

Frequently people are afraid of being alone, of confronting themselves in the silence of their own company. In an excellent chapter entitled "Notes for a Philosophy of Solitude" Merton boldly stated that all people are called to be solitary, at least to some degree. Too frequently, however, modern man fills his aloneness with diversions and systematic distractions. This leads to alienation and is reinforced by society which provides numerous "things" to do, and to occupy our time, so much so that we can avoid our own company for twenty-four hours a day. "The function of diversion is simply to anesthetize the individual as individual, and to plunge him in the warm, apathetic stupor of a collectivity which, like himself, wishes to remain amused."[12]

Through contemplation, a little time set apart, we begin the process of taking possession of our lives. Part of this process involves ridding ourselves of the domination of the "social image"—the one which society prescribes as beneficial and praiseworthy. The one who seeks solitude is able to renounce this social imagery and dare to be himself. It is not without risk, but it is also not without its great reward.

The social dimension of contemplation means that the contemplative can live in the world yet transcend its society and its false values. He seeks to discover his own unique identity and share it with others. He does not merely conform with the norms of society or its standards but attempts to live according to the basic Christian and human principles.

The contemplative and the person who practices the way of nonviolence can be seen by others as a prophet, a sign of contradiction, or a fool. To many he may appear to be a failure, an escapist, he who wastes precious time when he could be earning money, but the contemplative exists in confrontation with a world and with a time to which he feels compelled to protest. He is in the world but not totally of it. He is part of his time, but not bound by it.

This is the beauty and the paradox of Merton and his approach to contemplation. In solitude he rediscovered other people and the heart of the world. The paradox is that "true solitude draws us into communion with others, and true communion with others draws us to solitude." [13] Merton's task and vocation was to find others in solitude, and to encourage more people to do the same.

This approach to contemplation which Merton espoused was not without its critics, [14] but he continued to remind Christians of their responsibilities and how they might best achieve them. He tried to rouse a sleeping and apathetic world. He once wrote: "Most of the world is either asleep or dead. The religious people are, for the most part, asleep. The irreligious are dead." [15] He tried to stir people into a new way of acting and thinking, a more Christian and human way of living and relating to one another and to themselves. It was not an easy task, but once he realized its gravity he relentlessly pursued it with all his literary and personal strength.

Merton's concept of contemplation is not egocentric but is centered in Christ. Contemplation should lead a person from zeroing in on himself to centering in on Christ, the one true center of all. In contact with that center, then, at his deepest self, in communion with Christ, a person is in harmony with the inner truth of his being, which permits him to be fully what he is.

Thus we see again that contemplation leads to an intuitive consciousness of being and all Being. Contemplation puts us in contact with the center of our universe and with the Center of the Universe, Christ himself.

As Merton developed these ideas more in depth, he began to see the wisdom of the Zen masters and Eastern mystics. He especially was interested in the way they lead to the direct intuition of the ground of being, an interest he was to pursue until his death in 1968.

As long as we are drawn out of ourselves in thoughtless and ceaseless activity, the bane of modern people, we find it most difficult to know the rest and quiet and solitude so essential to true self-knowledge. Contemplation and solitude, then, are not luxuries but vital necessities if we are to transcend isolation and loneliness and come to term with our true identity.

To know who we are and to be able to relate humanly to the world around us requires an experience of our inner selves and our inner truth. This experience, Merton maintained, can be achieved even in our busy, active world through contemplation. His philosophy of contemplation is closely linked with his optimistic philosophy of man, which is in reality his own philosophy of life. The ramifications of this philosophy of life lead to a fully integrated person who is socially conscious and active, open to all people, nonviolent in action, and ultimately a peacemaker.

The truth about man, the truth to which he needs to respond in order to find his way out of the wilderness of confusion that he has become, is to be found within himself. This encounter with one's inner truth, and the consequent discovery of true self, requires the ability to discern the false images and conventions of society.

The essential condition for such liberation is solitude. The function of this solitude is to dissolve "the unreality of our vulnerable shell,"[16] thus permitting the revelation of the inner reality it conceals.

Merton does not impose this solitude on man as though it were simply a nice quality to add, rather he speaks of the recognition of "the radical and essential solitude of man."[17] This is a solitude which was assumed by Christ and which, in Christ, becomes mysteriously identified with the solitude of God. Merton continually insists that a man who does not experience solitude, or the condition of being "alone" has not discovered his true identity, his real self.

Being fully human, being a true person, involves the recognition and acceptance of one's "having" or "being" an incommunicable secret and solitude.[18] Such a recognition and acceptance is gained only by means of frequent intervals of time in which a person is able to see through the trivialities of society and perceive the inner truth of things and of himself.

To gain this kind of insight and self-recognition, one must set aside time consistently; it must be practiced seriously. Contemplation should become part of daily life. It requires the "wretched austerity of living in complete honesty, without convention and therefore without support."[19] This can be achieved once a person has been driven into the "desert" by disillusionment, aloneness, nothingness, and absurdity. Once in the desert of one's own heart a person begins to discover that he or she is, after all, a person; a person loved by God.

Contemplation and Contemporary Society

Thomas Merton was not naive. He was fully aware of the difficulties that would be encountered in attempting a way of contemplation in the modern world. More precisely, he did not advocate simply a way of contemplation, but a way of life which incorporated contemplation. Periods of contemplation were seen as an essential part of a total and full life.

Merton himself asked whether contemplation could still find a place in the world of technology and conflict which is ours today. He answered in the affirmative, not because he thought the social climate was favorable to the contemplative experience, but because of his conviction that "contemplation must be possible if man is to remain human."[20] He was confident that many people were aware that they could not achieve a direct experience of reality and of themselves exclusively through the measuring instruments, statistical analysis, or graphic representations of modern technology. Such an experience of reality required something more, something Merton called contemplation.

It is difficult to describe, talk, or write about contemplation; it is an intensely personal and private affair. Merton was aware of this difficulty when he wrote that a description of contemplation is as illusive and difficult as contemplation itself can often be. "It is not this, not that. Whatever you say of it, it is other than what you say."[21] Discussions of the contemplative experience demonstrate the limitations of language and conceptual systems. Merton himself turned to poetry and photography, to present vivid images of what he was trying to say.

Caution and restraint are key words in talking about the contemplative experience. Merton warned that "nothing is more repellent than a pseudoscientific definition of the contemplative experience."[22] He also pointed out that there was no adequate psychology of contemplation, although he, himself, often delved into the psychological ramifications of the contemplative experience.[23]

As illusive as it may be, contemplation is not simply an expansion of consciousness nor simply a new perception of the social dimensions of the world. Merton insisted that it was "a radical change in one's way of being and living, and the essence of this change is precisely a liberation from dependence on external means to external ends."[24] He further described this radical change as "the coalescence of life, knowledge, freedom, and love in a supremely simple intuition of the unity of all love, freedom, truth, and life in their source, which is God."[25]

The modern person in search of contemplation is seeking the same goal as the ancient mystic or the desert father, union with himself, his God, and other people. The contemporary contemplative, whether monk or lay person, strives to transcend the "split" in themselves and to heal the wounds of inner division and violence, the scars of the modern world.

From this perspective the solitary in the desert and the contemplative in Manhattan can be seen as healing in himself the divisive illnesses of the world. It starts with an individual but if spread to a community and a society the power it possesses is awesome. Merton wrote that the contemplative life of one person" . . . is simply the life of all manifesting itself in him . . . as the person deepens his own thoughts in silence he enters into a deeper understanding of and communion with the spirit of his entire people."[26]

Thus we can see that the person who practices contemplation, who sets aside time each day to be in contact with his deepest self, is actually able to transcend himself and his culture. In turn, he can experience a deep, underlying unity and oneness of being, the foundation for a life of peacefulness and nonviolence. It is the beginning of being fully oneself, fully human.

Contemplation is the beginning of true humanism, for a man cannot truly know his fellow man until he finds him in himself.[27] This implied for Merton that the normal result of being a Christian contemplative is that one begins to work for the betterment of his fellow man. The person who practices true contemplation inevitably becomes at least more interested, if not an activist, in social affairs and issues.

The contemplative in the world must strive to fill himself with the light and love of Christ and his Spirit. Once he has this hope and love, he must demonstrate the fruits of his contemplation by social action.[28] In this way, Merton presented the Christian method of contemplation as a social ethic of spontaneous charity and concern for all people. His hope was that all people should see each other as brothers and sisters.

This is a living out of the basic principle of Christianity that each person must recognize his need for everyone else and his obligation to serve everyone else. Merton contended quite bluntly that Christian charity is simply not present or possible in a person who is unconcerned about social justice and social issues.[29]

The person who practices contemplation sees reality with a vision and clarity which is impossible to a person who is totally immersed or submerged in the cares and exigencies of the dog-eat-dog world. This does not mean he is blind to injustice and sees everything through rose-colored glasses however. On the contrary, he has a heightened aware-ness that he is a member of the world of the bomb, racial strife and revolution, big business, hyped-up advertising, and a score of social injustices heaped upon him. But he does not despair.

The contemplative, instead, more than anyone else, feels that "it is a glorious destiny to be a member of the human race, though it is a race dedicated to many absurdities and one which makes many terrible mis-takes; yet with all that, God Himself gloried in becoming a member of the human race."[30]

In Merton's social philosophy of contemplation, a person is not only prepared for social action, but contemplation actually gives birth to social action by teaching the contemplative that he and his fellowman are one. Contemplation is a far cry from being an excuse for rejecting or escaping the world and its injustices. Merton viewed it as a social ethic that demanded the contemplative to understand and redeem the world.[31]

He recommended that monks open their monasteries for retreats and for counseling laypeople who wished to learn more about contempla-tion, affording them a place of quiet and an opportunity for real soli-tude. He explained that solitude can really be found anywhere, howev-er. The contemplative in the world should set aside a room or even just a corner where no one will find him, distrub him, or even notice him. There he should enter into himself and discover the ground of his own being. He should try never to change this place, as it will become a very special place. He should return to it often and spend time in prayer, reflection, peacefulness, and contemplation.[32]

It cannot be stressed enough how important Merton felt that this time for contemplation was for all people. Too many modern men and wom-en are fragmanted, alienated, and almost totally frustrated. Too many people are not able to cope with everyday situations, the hectic pace of the business world, and the pressures that surround so many from every side.

Merton did not offer contemplation as a panacea for all ills, or as an ersatz wonder drug. The achievement of the contemplative spirit is difficult. It demands patience, dedication, and determination. It requires concentration, an emptying of all superfluous distractions, and real effort. It does not come over night and may take a lifetime to accomplish. The way of contemplation which leads to the way of nonviolence is, however, an authentic way of life. It is not something one masters and then leaves behind. It is a quality which enhances personality and enriches one's appreciation of others and self; it becomes as dear as life itself.

The person who strives to live a contemplative life enters into the community with a more fully integrated personality, a living unity. The contemplative experience enables a person to live in harmony with life's trying situations by giving one an interior wholeness and integration and a solid basis for a life of nonviolence.

Merton talks about the person who has achieved final integration as one who has a unified vision and experience. The finally integrated person has experienced birth on a higher level and is able to transcend his problems, difficulties, and even culture. Merton wrote of this final integration, achieved through contemplation, as "a state of transcultural maturity far beyond mere social adjustment."[33]

Final integration implied for Merton a state of heightened insight and a potentiality for unusual creativity. The fully integrated person lives on a transcultural level and is truly "catholic" in the fullest sense of the word. Rather than being confused or scared by contradictory ideas and trends in society, the integrated person can unify ideas and discern truth because of his unique perspective.

The fully integrated person can take partial or contrasting views and unify them into a dialectic with insights that are complementary. With this approach he is able to, "bring perspective, liberty, and spontaneity into the lives of others. The finally integrated person is a peacemaker first and foremost, and that is why there is such a desperate need for our leaders to become such men of insight."[34]

Contemplation, therefore, for Thomas Merton is seen with numerous social dimensions and ramifications. Neither is it mysticism, pure and simple, nor is it prayer meant only for cloistered monks. It is the discovery and deepening of self and personality. It is the direct intuition of reality'' . . . the *simplex intuitus veritatis*, the pure awareness which is and must be the ground not only of all genuine metaphysical speculation, but also of mature and sapiental religious experience.''[35]

The fact that one pursues contemplation does not mean that a person is withdrawn from the world, or completely shut up. Rather, it implies a definite openness to the world and a genuine participation in its anguish and problems.

Awareness and openness are gifts, but they also normally presuppose the knowledge and practice of certain disciplines. Merton wrote that contemplation is both a ''gift'' and an ''art,'' albeit an almost ''lost art,'' as he himself admitted.[36]

The way of contemplation for Merton was a viable way by which people could experience unity and peace. It was a way of life and a way to greater life. It would enable men to be more fully human by being more fully themselves. It is an essential element and quality for anyone who would like to make the way of nonviolence an integral part of his life. Without experiencing a deep realization and awareness of self, which leads to inner unity and peace, one would find it extremely difficult, if not impossible, to bring peace and unity to others and to the world around them.

Contemplation and Zen

In the 1960s Merton became increasingly interested in Oriental philosophy and Eastern contemplative traditions. He felt that the spiritual and perhaps the physical survival of both the East and the West may well depend upon the rediscovery of Asian culture and religious values.[37] He believed that the great Asian cultures of India, Japan, and China should be studied in American colleges and universities alongside those of ancient Greece and Rome.[38]

Christianity could be enriched by Oriental religious thought. Merton pointed out that Christianity has always assimilated other cultures and that the universality essential to it implied a willingness to enter into dialogue with any culture. Western man, so often overinvolved and extended, has much to learn from the Eastern contemplative approach to life.

Merton saw the contemplative experience as the real common ground of sharing for this ecumenical dialogue. Both Christianity and the major Oriental religious philosophies look to the transformation of man's consciousness. Merton hoped that a real sharing would help in the general transformation of human consciousness.

Of particular significance were Buddhism and Zen. Merton felt that Zen was neither a religion nor a philosophy but a way of being in the world. The whole Zen approach to life is contemplative. This is especially important today at a point when the civilization of the West is furthest from the contemplative.[39] Merton described Zen as ". . . consciousness unstructured by particular form or particular system, a trans-cultural, trans-religious, trans-formed consciousness. It is therefore in a sense 'void.' But it can shine through this or that system, religious or irreligious, just as light can shine through glass that is blue, or green, or red, or yellow."[40]

For a while Merton had been developing the thesis that Christianity needed a new consciousness. He was critical of the prevalent consciousness based on the Cartesian conception. This approach encouraged man to be "a subject for whom his own self-awareness as a thinking, observing, measuring and estimating "self" is absolutely primary."[41] This leads to a ". . . solipsistic bubble of awareness—an ego-self imprisoned in its own consciousness, isolated and out of touch with other such selves in so far as they are all 'things' rather than persons."[42]

Merton advocated a more metaphysical consciousness, which takes its beginning from Being rather than ego-consciousness. One reason modern people finds contemplation so difficult is because our consciousness is "thing" orientated, even our thinking about ourselves. A consciousness open to Being and the intuition and experience of Being, on the contrary, would prepare people for the way of contemplation.

What is required of Christians ". . . is that they develop a completely modern and contemporary consciousness in which their experience as men and women of our century is integrated with their experience as children of God redeemed by Christ."[43]

Zen could be helpful in forming this new consciousness, or at least in indicating a direction because it was not directed to the self. Merton wrote that Zen is ". . . nondoctrinal, concrete, direct, existential, and seeks above all to come to grips with life itself, not with ideas about life, still less with party platforms in politics, religions, science, or anything else."[44]

Merton's central concern in his study of Zen and Eastern traditions was to understand the various ways in which people of different traditions have conceived the meaning and method of the "way" which leads to the highest levels of religious or metaphysical awareness. This pursuit confirmed Merton's advocacy of nonviolence as a life commitment rather than as a tactic or political approach.[45]

Zen is not a system, it simply is. It is more concerned with being than with propositions. It insists on concrete practice rather than on study or intellectual meditation. It is ". . . the ontological *awareness of pure being* beyond subject and object, an immediate grasp of being in its "suchness" and "thusness."[46]

Merton related the Zen insight to his own philosophy of person. He saw that Zen was at the same time a liberation from the limitations of the individual and empirical ego, and a discovery of one's original nature and true face. The Zen insight is not our awareness, "but Being's awareness of itself in us."[47]

The way of Zen is not a pantheistic submersion or loss of self in "nature" or the One. On the contrary, ". . . it is a recognition that the whole world is aware of itself in me, and that "I" am no longer my individual and limited self . . . my identity is to be sought not in that separation from all that is, but in oneness (indeed, 'convergence') with all that is."[48]

As interested as Merton was in Zen he never diluted his commitment to Christianity or the Christian approach to God and contemplation. He looked to Zen and the other great traditions hoping to learn from them and share in the values and experiences which they embodied. He condemned as irresponsible any syncretism that sought to identify all religious experience as equally true and supernatural.[49]

Merton was always careful in his analogies between Christianity and Zen to point out that Christianity is a matter of supernatural revelation while Zen seeks to penetrate the natural ontological ground of being. He viewed Zen more as a way of natural contemplation which could be helpful to modern people in attaining an intuitive and immediate experience of God and all being.[50]

During the last years of his life Merton was engaged in a profound investigation of the monastic experience, attempting to discover new truths in Buddhism, Zen, and Hinduism. It seemed that he was seriously considering working toward a kind of philosophical-theological synthesis between East and West. It would have been one more thesis in his continuing dialectical process in search of truth and unity and peace.

McInerny writes that Merton was working toward such an integration of Oriental thought, specifically Zen, into Christian philosophy and theology.[51] In the last years of his life, as his journey lead him to the East, Merton was subjecting various elements of Eastern thought to his own unique analysis and perspective. We were, unfortunately, due to his sudden death, never to see the full effect of the light which would have shone through the unique prism that was Thomas Merton's mind.

In his journey to the East, however, Merton has been called, by at least one writer, a "poor pilgrim".[52] Zen masters do not usually attempt to verbalize their experiences or write about the "ontological awareness of pure being." While he may have admired the Zen masters, Merton chose not to follow their lead in this regard. He attempted, on the contrary, to express in expository and philosophical terms what he had experienced in his journey inward.

As Malits points out, "Thomas Merton was a highly verbal Westerner impelled to speak about what he experienced or tried to understand. In that respect, he was a *poor* pilgrim. . . ."[53]

His continuing journey into the unknown, nonetheless had helped him to become more fully open to all peoples, traditions, and ideas. He grew progressively and dynamically in a dialogic process. His creative curiosity and utter faithfulness that God would walk with him every step of the way, no matter where or how far he traveled, are two more reflections of the legacy left by Merton, the pilgrim of peace who would not leave a stone unturned in his quest for the way of nonviolence.

Chapter III
The Way of Nonviolence

Throughout his adult life, Merton consistently maintained an antiwar mentality. As a Columbia undergraduate in the mid-1930s, he took the Oxford Pledge never to participate in any war. After his conversion to Catholicism in 1938, he acquainted himself with the Christian "just war" theory and began to question the Christians' involvement in any war.

The Vietnam war, which Merton referred to as "an overwhelming atrocity,"[1] served as the chief impetus for his speculation upon the Christian philosophy of war. With his usual dialectical approach, he treated the subjects of war and peace in numerous articles, essays, and books. He never formulated a tightly constructed, completely developed theory as such, but his writings taken together as a continuum form a philosophy, or better yet, a way of nonviolence, based upon his critique of war and search for peace.

Merton believed and stated unequivocally that "the root of all war is fear," not so much the fear men have of one another as "the fear they have of everything."[2] He stated as early as 1949 that ". . . it is not merely that they do not trust one another; they do not even trust themselves."[3]

In his presentation of fear and lack of trust as the core root of all war, Merton gives a view into his concept of contemporary man. He laments that if men are not sure when someone else may turn around and kill them, they are even less sure when they may turn around and kill themselves.[4]

People today cannot trust anything or anyone, and thus precipitate violence and war, because they have ceased to believe in God. In Merton's perspective, people who have become estranged from or have ceased to believe in God can never attain the fullness of humanity or their own destiny. A person does violence to his own inner nature when he denies, ignores, or only pays lip service to God. This, in turn, gives rise to violence in his dealings with other people, stemming from his own incompleteness, frustration, and disunity.

"It is not only our hatred of others that is dangerous but also and above all our hatred of ourselves."[5] This is especially true of that self-hatred which is often too deep and too powerful to be honestly confronted. This fear of confronting our own inner violence often compels us to project our violence on others. Sometimes this occurs under the guise of trying to destroy the evil in the other, but in reality we often end up destroying the other person, or country, in the process. Merton applied this interesting dynamic to the Vietnam conflict in relation to the American consciousness and society.

In the application of this psychology of war and violence to Vietnam, Merton maintained that our external violence was "rooted in an inner violence which simply ignores the human reality of those we claim to be helping."[6] He saw the essential evil of the Vietnam conflict stemming from the commitment to violence in utter disregard for the rights of the individuals the war had come to represent.

This basic fear and mistrust among people is also at the foundation of the arms race. Merton repeatedly condemned the arms race. In the mid-1960s he frequently quoted Pope John XXIII as a deeply religious and rational man who "deplored the gigantic stockpiles of weapons, the arms race and the cold war."[7]

Pope John XXIII was among the first world leaders to call the great powers to end the arms race and come ". . . to an agreement of a fitting program of disarmament, employing mutual and effective controls."[8]

Pope Paul VI was even more forceful in his statement presented in

June 1978 to the United Nations Special Session on Disarmament in which he gives the final objective as, ". . . completely eliminating the atomic arsenal." Pope Paul, like Merton, stated that ". . . the problem of disarmament is substantially a problem of mutual trust. . . ." And like Merton's prophetic warnings, the Pontiff added, ". . . tomorrow may be too late."[9]

Pope Paul VI stated, without hesitation, "There will be no disarmament of weapons if there is no disarmament of hearts."[10]

The social justice message issuing from the Vatican is clear and strong. It has, however, to a great degree fallen on deaf ears. Like Merton, the Holy See has sought to move men's hearts and awaken the consciences of Christians.

Pope John Paul II has constantly brought his message of peace forcefully and visibly to the world through his numerous trips and strong messages to all peoples.

The Pope's statement for the World Day of Peace, January 1, 1979, was entitled: "To Reach Peace, Teach Peace." This message in extremely Mertonian in its language and content. The Pope says that ". . . peace is something built up by everyone. . . . The great cause of peace between peoples needs all the energies of peace present in man's heart."[11] Pope John Paul II assures us that he takes the ". . . pilgrim's staff of peace. I am on the road, at your side, with the Gospel of peace."[12]

Pope John Paul II enumerates several principles for the attainment of peace which are very similar to those enunciated by Merton in his way of nonviolence. Among the principles the Pope states: "Human affairs must be dealt with humanely, not with violence." He calls for negotiation, not force, and a climate of open dialogue. A major principle reads: "Recourse to arms cannot be considered the right means for settling conflicts."[13] We shall treat this again in Merton's critique of the "just war" theory.

Although Merton was silenced for a while and forbidden to write or publish his views on Vietnam or war, the bishops in the United States have begun the attempt to educate their people for peace. On the occasion of the ordination of a new bishop for the Military Ordinariate, John Cardinal Krol of Philadelphia, condemned the "folly of the arms race"[14] by calling for a gradual disarmament. Cardinal Krol called the arms race "an act of aggression, because of the incalculable outpouring of economic resources and human energies, to the detriment of resources to schools, health, agriculture, and civil welfare."[15]

Merton asked the same question Cardinal Krol asked after the Philadelphia Cardinal cited current figures on armament spending and asked if such expenditures are not "a crime against God and man?"[16]

Merton saw the problem of violence coming not only from individuals but emanating from within the whole social structure ". . . which is outwardly ordered and respectable, and inwardly ridden by psychopathic obsessions and delusions."[17]

Merton presented some of the basic tenets of his social philosophy in an incisive essay entitled, "Toward a Theology of Resistance."[18] In his essay he strongly contended that theology today needs to focus more carefully upon the crucial problem of violence. Violence is closely interwoven with a society which itself is violent.

This violence within society is nourished by a brutal and convenient mythology "which simply legalizes the use of force by big criminals against little criminals—whose small-scale criminality is largely *caused* by the large-scale injustice under which they live. . . ."[19]

Merton derides the mythology of force which is "systematically kept in existence by the mass media," which presents nonviolence as being inadequate to cope with social problems. This is so because nonviolence is based on principles which call into question the popular self-understanding of the society in which we live.[20]

The societal influence on violence is traceable to the highly complex bands of organizations whose operations are global. Merton intended to defend the dignity and rights of people against, "The encroachments and brutality of massive power structures which threaten either to enslave him or to destroy him, while exploiting him in their conflicts with one another."[21]

Catholic moral theology and philosophy have fallen short of their responsibilities in adequately treating the complex questions of violence and war. Merton felt that these questions of social justice were among the crucial areas of theological investigation and should be the concern of society and philosophy.[22]

This does not mean, however, that he was calling for a pacifism which was denying all forcible resistance against unjust aggression. Often this is the only way, because as Pope John XXIII admitted, "unfortunately the law of fear still reigns among peoples."[23] This is especially true when the claims of the powerful and of the establishment are heavily favored against the common good or against the rights of the oppressed.

Merton's critique goes even further as he maintains that much of the violence today is white-collar violence; the systematically organized bureaucratic and technological destruction of people. The real problem is often not the individual with a gun but death and genocide as big business. We can just imagine the outcry from the monastery for the plight of the "boat people" refugees in the far East or of Lebanese civilians who indiscriminatly are being slaughtered. Merton constantly asked American Christians whether they were willing to accept responsibility for the worldwide activities of their country, in the areas of war, arms sales, big business, and exploitation.

The real crimes of modern warfare are committed as much on the front as they are in the war offices and ministries of defense. "Modern technological mass murder . . . is abstract, corporate, businesslike cool, free of guilt feelings and therefore a thousand times more deadly and effective than the eruption of violence out of individual hate."[24]

Contemporary society is violent, too, in the daily pressures and tensions that it brings to so many people. Even the idealist fighting for peace by nonviolent methods can easily succumb to this modern form of violence, viz., activism and overwork. The rush and pressure of modern life is a form, perhaps the most common form, of society's innate violence.

Merton innumerates some of the ways this can occur by allowing oneself to be carried away by a multitude of conflicting concerns, surrendering to too many demands, committing oneself to too many projects, wanting to help everyone and accomplishing nothing.[25] This style of life is tantamount to coopearation in violence and neutralizes one's work for peace. It destroys the inner capacity of the individual for peacefulness. It nullifies the fruitfulness of one's work, because it kills the root of inner wisdom and peaceful unity which makes work fruitful. Again, we see that what is needed is contemplation to restore unity, energize the individual from within and establish an inner peace from which all else will flow.

Another area in which Merton applied his analysis of society and presented his social philosophy of nonviolence as a solution was that of racism. He was in deep sympathy with the plight of many Black people in the United States. He saw their frustration as the result of much injustice in American society. He viewed the nonviolent protests of Martin Luther King, Jr., as one of the best and most effective uses of nonviolent philsophy and action in social and political issues.

The eventual turn to Black Power and violence, Merton attributed as much to the fact that American society would only heed violent actions and rhetoric as to the frustrations of the Black people.[26] Merton's views on racism will be discussed at greater length later.

We have seen that violence, according to Merton, stems from a basic disunity within man and within society. With this existential situation being such, men have traditionally established theories and limits justifying war in certain circumstances. We shall now consider Merton's view of this approach and his critique of it.

The "Just War" Theory and Pacifism

The principles of nonviolence which Thomas Merton developed were not the result of a detached contemplation divorced from the world, but arose from his acute sensitivity to the evils and dangers plaguing the world and all people. One reason he felt compelled to foster the pursuit of nonviolence was the inadequacy of the traditional "just war" theory to meet the exigencies of modern warfare. He also felt it necessary to speak in true Gospel terms to contemporary Christians.

The position of Origen and other early Church Fathers, such as Clement of Alexandria, Justin Martyr, and St. Cyprian, was that Christians should not take up arms in any war. This seems to have been the official position of the Church in the first four centuries. Origen wrote: "Christians have been taught not to defend themselves against their enemies; and because they have kept the laws which command gentleness and love of man, on this account they have received from God that which they would not have succeeded in doing if they had been given the right to make war, even though they may have been quite able to do so."[27]

Celsus, a pagan traditionalist, attacked Christianity as being subversive of the old religious and social order. His chief grievance against the Christians, was ". . . their claim to . . . a special revealed truth . . . and in particular they refuse to fight in the army."[28]

In refuting Celsus, Origen gave some of the earliest Christian teaching on war and civil disobedience. The opening lines of *Contra Celsum* declare that it is not only right but obligatory to disobey human laws and ignore human customs when these are contrary to the law of God. Among other things, the Christians were united against war, in obedience to Christ. This was one of their chief differences with the rest of society.[29]

Merton quotes Origen who wrote: "No longer do we take the sword against any nations nor do we learn war any more since we have become the sons of peace through Jesus. . . ."[30]

Christians should refuse military service, but this does not mean that they do not bear their fair share of the common good and responsibilities. They exercise their role in a spiritual and transcendent way. They should help by their prayers, not by force of arms. Origen contends that these prayers will help the cause of peace more effectively than arms ever will.[31]

Merton concurs with Origen's reasoning when he argues that prayers are weapons in a more hidden, yet more crucial, type of warfare. He talks about a type of "warfare on" which a true lasting peace of the Empire or State more truly and certainly depends.

Here again, Merton avoids getting overly specific or too particular, but goes to the heart of the matter. He prefers to talk about rectifying the core root of all wars, rather than this or that particular war. "The weapon of prayer," he states, "is not directed against other men, but against the evil forces which divide men into warring camps."[32] In other words, Merton encourages the Christian to fight against war itself and its root causes with spiritual weapons, rather than fighting in this or that particular war with weapons of death.

Merton has been criticized for this approach, which to many seems too unrealistic, especially in a world in which the Communist threat spills over into one country after another. Merton did not deny that his approach might be unrealistic, but he often asked whether stockpiling nuclear weapons was really any more realistic an approach.

In analyzing the theory of the "just war" and the stance of the contemporary Church on war, Merton traced the historical development in the period between Origen's *Contra Celsum* and Augustine's *City of God*. He points out two significant events which radically changed the Christian approach to war. The first event was the proclamation of Christianity as the "official religion" of the Roman Empire by Constantine in the year 312. This followed the famous Battle of the Milvian Bridge.

The second key event was the march of Alaric the Goth on the city of Rome in the year 411. Seeing a parallel in Augustine's own life, Merton states that Augustine laid the foundation for Christian theories of the "just war," when the barbarians were at the gates of his own city of Hippo, where he was bishop.[33]

It is easy to see parallels today in our own country with an increased militaristic spirit and increased spending on defense and arms, to heights never before dreamed of.

We cannot go into much detail here about Augustine's idea of the human commonwealth with its two cities, the City of God and the earthly City. Very briefly, however, the City of God was governed by *caritas*, an unselfish love; and the earthly City by the *amor concupiscentiae*, the love of power and possession.[34]

The problem stems from the fact that these cities are not separate from one another. The Christian with his *caritas* must live in the city where the *concupiscentiae* flourishes. All societies should seek peace, but in the earthly City war is not entirely unavoidable; and if it wages war, it should do so for the sake of peace. Then, according to Augustine, the Christian has the right to fight in that war to protect the earthly City.[35]

Merton is critical of this stance that the Christian has the right or the obligation to wage a war for whatever reason. The key factor in Augustine's theory is that the Christian is not really defending the earthly City, but is waging a war to establish peace. Thus it is the interior motive which justifies war: the love of peace to be safe-guarded by necessary force. In this view violence is sanctioned through the purity of intention. Augustine does not say the Christian must enter such a war but that he *may* enter. Nevertheless, Augustine seems to encourage him to do so.[36]

On the one hand, then, we have Origen whose world view was eschatological, looking to the end-time. He takes for granted that the Christian is called to be and wants to be a peacemaker. On the other hand, we have Augustine with a much more pragmatic and moralistic world view who states that a Christian could enter into a war for the sake of peace.[37] Merton quotes Augustine, almost in dismay as saying: "Love does not exclude wars of mercy waged by the good."[38]

The situation which confronted Augustine was that of a collapsing Empire being shattered and attacked on all sides by barbarian armies. It seemed that war could not be avoided. The task that confronted him was to find some way to fight that did not seem to violate the law of love.

Augustine reconciled war with Christian love, by going back to pre-Christian, classical notions of justice, particularly that of Cicero, and justified the use of force for a just cause. Again Merton cites Augustine: "If one's interior motive is purely directed to a just cause and to love of the enemy, then the use of force is not unjust."[39] The war, however, had to be a just war with a limited amount of cruelty.

St. Thomas Aquinas synthesized the conditions for war scattered throughout Augustine's writings and then added a fourth of his own. Thus for a war to be just, first, the authority of the sovereign by whose command the war is waged must be legitimate. Second, a just cause is required. Third, it is necessary that the belligerents have a rightful intention. Fourth, the right use of means.[40] It should be noted that Merton did not specifically treat this aspect of Thomas' thought, although he did quote both Pope John XXIII and Pope Paul VI regarding nuclear weapons used in war.

Merton called Augustine, "for better or for worse, the Father of all modern Christian thought on war."[41] One of the weaknesses Merton saw built into Augustine's theory was the subjective nature of acting out of one's good intentions, where the danger of rationalization is so high. Merton likewise lamented the fact that there were no limits to the amount of violence inflicted in the interest of or the name of justice and cited examples from the times of the Christian Crusades.

Pope John Paul II in his recent encyclical on the mercy of God, *Dives in Misericordia* discusses what violence has been purpetrated in the name of justice. Sounding very much like Merton who wrote twelve years before, Pope John Paul II writes how a neighbor is sometimes destroyed, killed, deprived of liberty, or stripped of fundamental human rights "in the name of alleged justice (for example, historical justice or class justice)."[42]

The deficiency of Augustinian thought, Merton felt, was not so much in the good intentions that it prescribed but "in an excessive naiveté with regard to the good that can be attained by violent means which cannot help but call forth all that is worst in man."[43] Merton held that Augustine's pessimism about human nature and the world was often used as a *justification* for recourse to violence.[44]

Merton made a strong plea for a re-evaluation of the "just war" theory in light of modern warfare and especially nuclear warfare. He noted that if there were to be significant new developments in Christian thought on nuclear war, it may depend on our ability to get free from some of the overpowering influence of Augustinian assumptions of man, society, and war itself. Merton believed that nuclear war was qualitatively different than tradition forms of warfare and should be discussed in this new light.

Merton concurred with Pope John XXIII and Pope Paul VI that today there is a new kind of war, "one in which the old concept of the "just war" is irrelevant because the *necessary conditions for such a war no longer exist*. A war of total annihilation simply cannot be considered a "just war" no matter how good the cause for which it is undertaken."[45]

American Catholics, for the most part, Merton chides, are a passive unit in the affluent mass society who consecrate the values of the secular society. It is time to wake up and to activate the consciences in this matter of war and peace. "The only sane course," he declared, "is to work frankly and without compromise for the total abolition of war."[46]

In assessing the critical urgency on the practical level, Merton asserted that each Christian has a duty, as a Christian" . . . to contribute everything he can to help this great common work: of finding non-military and nonviolent ways of defending our rights, our interests, and our ideals."[47]

While it appeared to many at the time he was writing in the 1960s, that Merton had an exaggerated anxiety over the dangers and threat of nuclear war, recent developments have proven him to have been dead on target. *Time* magazine in its cover story titled, "Thinking the Unthinkable, Rising Fears about Nuclear War," talks about living with the possibility of mega-death.[49] This article discusses the new movement across the United States in the early 1980s, which includes "more bishops than Berrigans, doctors and lawyers . . ." all of whom are advocating nuclear disarmament.[50] The movement aims at achieving what Merton worked so hard to accomplish in the 1960s, namely an awareness of the horrors of war and a nonviolent form of protest. Once again Merton was in the forefront of a movement which has taken a generation to mature and mobilize.

Merton constantly tried to awaken Christians to their own moral obligations and to the enormity of the present situation, which, of course, exists even more dangerously in the eighties than it did in the mid-1960s when he was writing. Taking his lead from the pronouncements of the Holy See, especially those of Pope John XXIII, he declared that the "only sane course that remains is to work frankly and without compromise for the total abolition of war."[51]

All recent Pontiffs, he noted, have pointed in this direction as the only ultimate, moral, and sane solution. All Christians, however, have the duty to help clarify thought on this issue by taking the stand "that all-out nuclear, bacterial, or chemical warfare is unacceptable as a practical solution in international problems because it would mean the destruction of the world."[52]

He acknowledged that it is the unanimous judgment of all really serious religious, philosophical, social, and psychological thought today that *total war* (whether nuclear or conventional) is both immoral and suicidal. Even theologians, both Catholic and non-Catholic, who insist that "war itself can still be resorted to as a solution to international conflicts, and who therefore recommend strong military measures of defense, agree in practice that total war must be condemned not only as immoral but also as impractical and self-defeating."[53]

In assessing the critical urgency on the practical level, Merton asserted that each Christian has a duty, specifically as a Christian, ". . . to contribute everything he can to help this great common work: of finding non-military and nonviolent ways of defending our rights, our interests, and our ideals."[54]

Although the actual threat of nuclear wat itself may not always be imminent, the current "balance of power," or more properly the "balance of terror," which exists in the world between the superpowers is maintained, albeit precariously, by huge stockpiles of weapons, many of which are nuclear. The senseless arms race, which now has spread to many Third World countries is like an uncontrolled world going downhill without brakes.

This extremely dangerous situation, Merton writes, is due to societal irresponsibility on the moral level, in addition to, what he calls demonic activism in social, military and political life.[55] Merton advocated making every effort to negotiate a multilateral disarmament agreement.

He was realistic and politically astute enough not to advocate a radical and sweeping policy of "unilateral disarmament." It would have been naive, and possibly could do more harm than good. He foresaw that the state of shock in which millions of people already live, might be magnified thousands of times over if their "only means of defense" were suddenly taken away—a situation which itself might precipitate a war.

On the other hand, he strongly proposed "unilateral initiatives in gradual steps toward disarmament" as being imperative.[56] But even such limited steps imply a strength of belief in effective alternatives to military defense and this brings us back to the question of the methods of nonviolence.[57]

In formulating his Christian ethic and social philosophy on the issues of war and peace, Merton took particular pains to enunciate what he was not. On numerous occasions he emphatically declared that he was not a pacifist, at least in the traditional sense.

Merton did not like himself to be called a pacifist because of the many ambiguities in the term pacifism. He likewise did not appreciate the facile caricature of the "pacifist" as a "maladjusted creature lost in impractical ideas, sentimentally hoping that prayer and demonstrations can convert men to the ways of peace."[58] He also disliked certain fundamental religious ambiguities which he saw in pacifism, which could leave it open to manipulation and misinterpretation.

Any pacifism which was rooted in a world-denying or overly individualistic asceticism was shunned by Merton. A type of pacifism which regards war as an inevitable yet intolerable evil in corrupt world from which it cannot be separated, and which the individual believer must renounce, is totally against Merton's view.[59]

Equally unacceptable is a form of pacifism that tends, as a cause, to take on the air of a quasi-religion, as though it were a kind of faith in its own right. In this context he fears the Christian pacifist who insists that pacifism is an integral part of Christianity and concludes that Christians who are not pacifists have, by that fact, apostatized from Christianity.[60]

In accord with Pope John XXIII Merton preferred the term "peace-maker" to that of "pacifist" and concurred with the Pope that being a "peacemaker" meant more and demanded more, not less, than being a "pacifist."

Many of the current modes of thought and approach involving the crucial issue of war and arms were ruled inadequate in Merton's evalua-tion of the conventional "pacifist" position.[61] In a typical strain of striving for the ideal, Merton felt that the pursuit of nonviolent means to resolve conflict was not purely a matter of individual conscience alone, but involved all peoples as a worldwide social question.

In view of the enormous danger represented by nuclear weapons and the near impossibility of controlling and limiting them Merton was led to admit a relative pacifism. Because the improbability of controlling nuclear weapons "to a scale that would fit the traditional ethical theory of a just war," Merton said, "makes it both logical and licit for a Catholic to proceed, from motives of conscience, to at least a relative pacifism, and to a policy of nuclear disarmament."[62]

While Merton repeatedly emphasized the fact that he was not a paci-fist and did not hold that the Christian was forbidden ever to fight or that no war could ever be just, his reasoning here was more on the level of theory for him than on the level of practice and actuality. Although it can be argued that, even on the level of theory, one can find hints of inconsistency in his discussion of pacifism and the just war "which suggest that his heart really did belong to the former and his fervent protestations to the contrary were largely a matter of semantics."[63]

He rejected a pacifism that was total or absolute and a peace move-ment that was superficial. His was rather a position that left room, in theory at least, for a defensive war against an unjust aggressor. It must be emphasized, however, that this was *in theory.* In practice Merton was against all war.

Brother Patrick Hart, Merton's long-time friend and secretary at Gethsemani Abbey, in the Prologue to this book, calls him a "nuclear pacifist . . . who was dedicated wholeheartedly to nonviolence as the only way of achieving peace."[64]

Merton regarded the current war ethic as pagan and fully concurred with Pius XII that "*total war* must be condemned."[65] The italicized reference to "total war" provides, perhaps, the key by which the apparent inconsistency in Merton's position on peace and pacifism can be understood. Zahn writes that Merton was a pacifist "in that he rejected the legitimacy of war in . . . actuality."[66]

He was convinced that total war, and specifically nuclear war, would have to be immoral in fact. He was equally afraid that any war could easily escalate to the level of nuclear war. He was unalterably opposed to all war and dedicated himself to bringing about the elimination of all weapons and the excessive reliance placed upon them by the superpowers.[67]

"The present war crisis," Merton wrote, "is something we have made entirely for and by ourselves. There is in reality not the slightest logical reason for war, and yet the whole world is plunging headlong into frightful destruction, and doing so *with the purpose of avoiding war and preserving peace!* This is true war-madness, an illness of the mind and spirit that is spreading with a furious and subtle contagion all over the world."[68] Never one to understate his argument, Merton goes on to add, "Of all the countries that are sick, America is perhaps the most greviously afflicted."[69]

What is the role to be played by the Christian in light of this situation? Merton insists that he is no prophet, but talks about the futility of building bomb shelters, "where, in case of nuclear war (we) will simply bake slowly instead of burning quickly or being blown out of existence in a flash. . . . Truly we have entered the "post-Christian era" with a vengeance. Whether we are destroyed or whether we survive, the future is awful to contemplate."[70]

We can imagine Merton's outrage directed against the Reagan administration's proposal for a seven-year, $4.2 billion project for evacuating 319 urban target areas in the United States in the event of threatened nuclear attack.[71] In October 1981, the Civil Defense chief of Idaho Falls conducted a trial exercise in this multibillion dollar "get-out-of-town project." He was quoted as saying, "Our position is that the United States must perceive and address nuclear war as 'thinkable' and structure our strategic force levels and Civil Defense accordingly."[72]

Thus Merton's prophetic stance cuts to the quick even more so today than in the 1960s. His worst fears seem to be materializing with an amazing haste. As he frequently stated, "Christians have a grave responsibility to protest clearly and forcibly against trends that lead inevitably to crimes which the Church deplores and condemns. Ambiguity, hesitation and, compromise are no longer permissible. 'War must be abolished!' "[73]

With this as the urgent challenge which Merton issued to confront the Christian conscience let us turn to a consideration of his alternative to war and violence—the Christian ethic of nonviolence. First we shall consider its classic form, espoused by Mahatma Gandhi, and accepted by Merton.

Gandhi and Nonviolence

No adequate understanding of Thomas Merton's Christian ethic of nonviolence is possible without an appreciation of the nonviolence taught and lived by Mahatma Gandhi. For Merton, Gandhi embodied the basic principles of the way of nonviolence and pointed the way to the uncompromising commitment demanded by the practice of true nonviolence. For Gandhi, the way of nonviolence demanded more bravery than fighting in war or dying in battle.

Without going into detail about the historical circumstances in which Gandhi formulated his way of nonviolence, we will discuss here the basic tenets of his approach as seen by Merton and the influence they had on Merton.

In a lengthy and challenging introduction to his book on Gandhi, Merton gives his own assessment and evaluation of Gandhi's life and his principles of nonviolence. Merton once referred to Gandhi as "a model of integrity we cannot afford to ignore,"[74] and went so far as to say he felt that it was almost a basic duty for all peoples to imitate Gandhi, especially in dissociating ourselves from evil in the world.

Gandhi received a completely Western education as a young man, and it was through the West that he really discovered the East. Although he thought and acted like an Englishman, he discovered something universal in the new suit of Western man that he found himself wearing. Through his acquaintance with writers like Tolstoy and Thoreau, and through his reading of the New Testmant, Gandhi rediscovered his own traditions and his Hindu *dharma*.[75]

In a sense Gandhi discovered India in discovering himself. This discovery of self is a key factor in a proper understanding of Gandhi's nonviolence and his political life. In light of this radical discovery, Merton maintained everything else received its meaning.

Merton described this discovery by Gandhi as a realization "that the people of India were awakening in him. . . . It was the spiritual consciousness of a people that awakened in the spirit of one person."[76] The message of this Indian spirit, however, was not for India alone, but rather for the entire world. It represented, in a sense, the "awakening of a new world."

For Gandhi then, ". . . the spirit of nonviolence sprang from an inner realization of spiritual unity in himself. The whole Gandhian concept of nonviolent action and *satyagraha* is comprehensible if it is thought to be as the *fruit of inner unity already achieved* rather than a means of achieving unity."[77]

This aspect of inner unity which is so much a part of the nonviolence of Gandhi and Merton enables it to become a spiritual and religious humanism. The way of nonviolence is an authentic philosophy of life and social ethic based on a view of man that is essentially optimistic and (at least potentially) Christian.

Gandhi neither accepted nor rejected Christianity, but he took from it all that he found to be relevant to him as a Hindu. Merton wrote that "Gandhi had the deepest respect for Christianity, for Christ, and the

Gospel. In following his way of nonviolence (*satyagraha*) he believed he was following the Law of Christ."[78]

Gandhi's knowledge and appreciation of Christianity was more than passing. "His standard was the standard of the New Testament. He attempted to do all things as in the name of Christ, in the name of truth. . . ."[79]

Not only did Gandhi know the New Testament thoroughly, but Merton believed that he was ". . . one of the very few men of our time who applied Gospel principles to the problems of a political and social existence in such a way that his approach to these problems was inseparably religious and political at the same time."[80]

Gandhi coined the word *satyagraha* to describe his philosophy of nonviolent dedication to truth. *Satyagraha* was a religious and spiritual force, a wisdom born of fasting and prayer. True *satyagraha* often involves a vow to die rather than say what one does not mean. *Satyagraha* meant first of all refusing to say "nonviolence" and "peace" when one really meant "violence" and "destruction."[81]

As with so many of Gandhi's tenets, *satyagraha*, the holding on to truth, should reach out into the public forum. It involves a process of educating the public and forming public opinion. Satyagraha is never vindictive or destructive rather it strives for conversion. If it fails it is due to the one who practices it rather than to the principle of *satyagraha* itself.[82]

This conversion and social aspect is one which Merton integrates into his ethic of nonviolence as an essential element. For both men nonviolence as a way of life demands that one who practices and lives it, "is totally dedicated to the transformation of his own life, of his adversary, and of society."[83]

One of the aspects of Gandhi's nonviolence which Merton admired most was his total dedication to truth. Gandhi was more concerned with truth and service than with success or recognition. Two statements from Gandhi sum up his whole doctrine of nonviolence: "The way of peace is the way of truth" and "truthfulness is even more important than peacefulness."[84]

Gandhi's whole religio-political action was based on an ancient metaphysic of man, a philosophical wisdom common to Hinduism, Buddhism, Islam, Judaism, and Christianity: "truth is the inner law of our being."[85]

The person who follows the way of nonviolence must strive to attain an intuition of being, both in man and in the world, so that a vow of truth is also a vow of fidelity to being in all its dimensions. Hence "the way of peace is the way of truth, of fidelity to wholeness and being, which implies a basic respect for life, not as a concept, not as a sentimental figment of the imagination, but in its deepest most secret and most frontal reality."[86]

This correlation of the spirit of truth with the spirit of nonviolence was one of the deepest insights that Merton gained from his study of Gandhi. It implies an openness in all situations and in all peoples to a possible conversion to the good and a progression from the way of peace, to the way of truth, to the way of nonviolence.

Merton quotes Gandhi as saying that "Truth is God . . . which enables me to see God face to face as it were. I feel Him pervade every fiber of my being."[87] And Merton himself, not too long before his untimely death emphatically stated, "Nonviolence is not for power but for truth. It is not pragmatic but prophetic. It is not aimed at immediate political results, but at the manifestation of fundamental and crucially important truth."[88]

An optimistic view of human nature was shared by both Gandhi and Merton, and they held that truth was indeed the law of our being. We cannot fully appreciate their commitment to nonviolence without a grasp of their basic optimism regarding human nature. Gandhi believed that ". . . in the hidden depths of our being . . . we are more truly nonviolent."[89]

It is because of this strong relation between truth and nonviolence that both men were so strongly opposed to lying, which Merton referred to as the mother of violence. They taught that the lie brings violence and disorder into human nature itself. It divides people against themselves and alienates them from themselves. This inner division then gives rise to hatred and violence. Men hate others because they cannot stand the disorder and division they experience within. This, of course, is why Merton advocates a contemplation which leads to inner unity and a spirit of nonviolence.

"We are violent to others," Merton said, "because we are already divided by the inner violence of our infidelity to our own truth. Hatred projects this division outside ourselves into society."[90]

Another area in which Merton agreed with the approach of Gandhi was one's philosophical outlook on evil, and the role that evil played in the world and in the individual's life. Merton stated that all modern tyrannies have in one way or another emaphasized the irreversibility of evil in order to build their power upon it.

He cites Hitler as an example of one who firmly believed in the unforgivableness of sin, which became fundamental to the whole mentality of Nazism. "Hitler's world was built on the central dogma of the irreversibility of evil."[91]

Even the arguments of Adolph Eichmann, who pleaded obedience to his superiors, suggest a deep faith in an irreversible order which could not be changed, but only obeyed. For Hitler there was no place for the Jews, so the acts which eliminated them were irreversible. Hitler was a success in at least one thing: "everything he did bears the stamp of complete and paranoid finality."[92]

This view of evil is in direct contrast to that of St. Thomas Aquinas who views evil as reversible, and as the proper motive for mercy and compassion. For St. Thomas sin itself is already a punishment, and we in turn "feel sorrow and compassion for the sinners."[93]

Merton taught that we must possess the interior strength to assume the suffering of another and our own and thus change the condition of the other by forgiveness and acceptance. A person must first be able to admit both defect and fallibility before it is possible to become merciful to others.

A refusal to accept the precariousness and the risk that is part of all finite good in this life leads to the belief in the finality and irreversibility of evil. Merton admits that the good that people do is always in the realm of the uncertain and the fluid, and that love triumphs in this life, not by eliminating evil once and for all but by resisting and overcoming it anew every day. This is one of the basic reasons for the difference in approach between the violence of war which seeks to destroy the enemy (seen as evil) and the nonviolent approach which seeks to win them over, because there is good even in an enemy.

A true nonviolent way of life takes this dynamic, evolving element of society into account. The nonviolent person sees the ". . . . dynamic and non-final state of all relationships among men, for nonviolence seeks to change relationships that are evil into others that are good, or at least less bad."[94]

Nonviolence then, does not seek to destroy the evil, or oppressor, or eliminate it by force, rather it seeks to convert or transform it to good. To punish or destroy an oppressor, Merton held, is merely to initiate a new cycle of violence and oppression. The only real liberation is that which liberates both the oppressor and the oppressed. This too was held by Gandhi who believed that the highest form of spiritual freedom was to be sought in the strength of heart which is capable of liberating the oppressed and oppressor together. This concept with all its important consequences is an integral part of the foundation of Merton's view of nonviolence.

The vision of evil is part of the core of the way of nonviolence. A nonviolent approach will stand or fall depending on the stance taken regarding evil. If evil is seen as irreversible then the only recourse is violence and destruction. But when evil is seen as reversible, it can be turned into forgiveness, and then nonviolence becomes a possibility.[95]

Since Merton had experienced forgiveness through Christ in his own personal life, then nonviolence becomes not only a possibility but an integral part of being Christian. Merton firmly agreed with Gandhi who wrote: "The business of every god-fearing man is to . . . have faith in a good deed producing only a good result. . . . He follows the truth, though following of it may endanger his very life. He knows that it is better to die in the way of God than to live in the way of Satan."[96]

Merton saw that Gandhi's principles were pertinent in the 1960s for any who was interested in implementing the principles expressed by Pope John XXIII in *Pacem in Terris*. He felt that this encyclical had the breadth and depth, the universality and tolerance, of Gandhi's own peace-minded outlook. Peace, Merton wrote, cannot be built on exclusivism, absolutism, and intolerance. There can be no peace on earth without the kind of inner change that brings man back to his "right mind."[97]

Gandhi exerted a powerful influence over Merton and his formulation of his own Christian philosophy of nonviolence. We shall now consider another person who greatly influenced Merton—Pope John XXIII and specifically his encyclical *Pacem in Terris* which re-enforced Merton's optimistic point of view in his way of nonviolence.

Chapter IV
Pacem in Terris and the Principles of Nonviolence

The views of Pope John XXIII exerted a strong influence over the "mature" Thomas Merton who was agonizing over questions of war and peace. Merton took up the challenge which Pope John XXIII issued to all Christians. He welcomed Pope John's attitude and began to reflect it in his own writings.

Merton was, in fact, so impressed by Pope John's encyclical letter *Pacem in Terris,* issued in 1963, that he was moved to write an "official" interpretation and response to it. He wrote that the real question facing the "dwindling and confused Christian minority in the West" was not whether they *could* do anything to improve world conditions, as the Pope commanded, but what they actually *intended* to do.[1] He believed along with Pope John that Christians could have a great influence if they only tried to exercise the powers which they already possessed. They must overcome their fear and hesitancy to speak out, they must be aware, they must be awakened.

For Merton the whole basis of Pope John's encyclical is found in the rights and dignity of the human person. The person finds a reason for existence in the realm of truth, justice, love, and liberty. He fulfills himself ". . . not by closing himself within the narrow confines of his own individual interests and those of his family, but by his openness to other men, to the civil society in which he lives and to the society of nations in which he is called to collaborate with others in building a world of security and peace.''[2]

It is necessary to distinguish between person and individual. ''The individual can be considered as an isolated human unit functioning and acting for himself and by himself.''[3] The person, on the other hand, can never be understood properly outside the framework of social relationships and obligations. The person does not exist merely to fight for survival: man is not a ''gorilla with a gun.''[4]

Pacem in Terris in its discussion of authority criticizes current failures of authority in the national and international sphere for either exercising it without regard for Christian principles, or without sufficient regard for the common good. In characteristic style Merton approaches the vital question of authority by contrasting the view of Machiavelli, which he says is the basis of much practice today, with that of Pope John.

Merton quotes Machiavelli: ''. . . There are two methods of fighting, one by law and the other by force. The first method is that of men, the second of beasts; but as the first method is often insufficient, one must have recourse to the second.''[5]

Somewhat cynically himself, Merton said that it would be ''instructive'' to read Machiavelli today and see ''how his pragmatic, not to say cynical, doctrine on the importance and the conduct of war are precisely those which are accepted in practice today in the international power struggle.''[6]

The Prince, says Machiavelli, should have ''no other aim or thought but war.''[7] He should be aware that disarmament would only render him contemptible, and he must never learn to be too good. For Machiavelli, power is an end in itself. Persons and policies are simply a means to that end, and the chief means is war, not a 'just war' but a *victorious* war. For Machiavelli the important thing was to *win*.''[8]

Authority in Machiavelli rests on ''force and ruse, ruthlessness and cruelty, the ability to seize power and hold on to it against all contenders.''[9] This viewpoint, Merton said, was quite commonly held and shared by many government leaders and countries.

Authority in *Pacem in Terris,* on the other hand, ". . . rests on the objective reality of man, on the natural law, that is on the inner orientation of man to freedom, and on the obligations which this entails."[10]

Pope John XXIII tirelessly repeated the principle that force is not and cannot be the valid basis for any authority over another person. Any civil authority that relies chiefly upon threats and fear of punishment cannot effectively promote the common good.

The Pontiff takes this principle further by stating that people and nations are right in not yielding obedience to authority imposed by force, or any authority in whose creation they had no part or choice.[11]

Pacem in Terris has as one of its basic tenets the fact that civil authority must appeal primarily to the conscience of the individual citizens. Authority can do this and exercise a rightful appeal to the conscience of men if it offers them some convincing indication that it can provide them with an ordered and productive life, with liberty and the advantages of a peaceful culture.[12]

The Pope concludes his argumentation by showing that the "ultimate source and final end of all authority" is God himself.[13] Merton concurred with this and often stated that the proper basis for authority is reason and conscience, guided by the fundamental principle of love.

Pacem in Terris also laid the moral foundation for the Catholic position of conscientious objection, which Merton firmly supported. Merton quotes Pope John: "those therefore who have authority in the State may oblige men in conscience only if their authority is intrinsically related to the authority of God and shares in it."[14]The encyclical goes on to say that it follows that if civil authorities pass laws or command anything opposed to the moral order and consequently contrary to the will of God neither the laws made, nor the authorization granted can be binding on the consciences of citizens.

Merton summarizes his analysis of Pope John's great social encyclical thus: "Pope John teaches that when authority ignores natural law, human dignity, human rights, and the moral order established by God, it undermines its own foundations and loses its claim to be obeyed because it no longer speaks seriously to the conscience of free man."[15]

One very serious consequence flows from this teaching, namely the failure of authority to cope with the critical needs and desperate problems of man on a world scale. This, Pope John said, and Merton agreed, was one of the great collective questions of conscience of our time.

From his own meditation upon this encyclical, Merton saw some deeply Christian obligations emerge in light of the world crisis of his day. He enumerated the following obligations: (1) to work for collaboration and harmony among nations; (2) to respect the rights of small and emergent nations and of racial minorities; (3) to collaborate actively and generously in helping these nations and races to attain their full development; (4) to work for peace; and (5) the need for a clear and forthright protest of the Christian conscience against the abuse of authority. All of this implies a willing and intelligent participation of the Christian in civil and public life,[16] a task to which Merton devoted much of his writing and later life.

Merton was convinced that the essential difference between the authority of love and truth taught by Pope John, as opposed to the brute force espoused by so many around the world, was rooted in a profoundly different concept of man and of the world. A totalitarian and absolute concept of authority, which is based on force and fear, implied a pessimistic view of man and of the world. This approach to authority suppresses the deepest values in man and is distrustful and fearful of real liberty and freedom. This kind of authority believes that "nature must be controlled with an iron hand because it is evil or prone to evil."[17] This is closely related to the belief in the irreversibility of evil that we discussed earlier.

Needless to say, Merton was diametrically opposed to such a pessimistic world view and consistently advocated a more Christian, optimistic vision that was open to all peoples and diverse ideas and beliefs. Pope John XXIII, too, was passionately opposed to this kind of pessimism, which he diagnosed as a sickness akin to despair. Merton liked to say that Pope John "dared to hope in the goodness placed in human nature by God the Creator."[18] Only if human nature is seen as radically good can a valid concept of authority based on natural law and human liberty be a guiding principle, eventually to become a reality.

Merton also compared the likeness of Pope John's optimism with that of St. Thomas Aquinas. Through his great synthesis of theology, St. Thomas united the created and uncreated, nature and grace, reason and faith in a vast and all-encompassing unity. Pope John and Merton, like St. Thomas before them, considered things to be good—all things. What is, is good because it was created by God.[19]

Without an understanding of this optimistic world view held by Pope John and so intimately shared by Merton, the Christian way of non-violence can seem to be as incomprehensible as it sometimes appears to be impractical. Without a firm basis in a deep Christian faith of a radically redeemed world and a forgiven mankind, then Merton's way of nonviolence is nothing more than the "fool's way" and "coward's path" that many opponents and non-believers think it is. This Christian optimism is not a vapid and sentimental kind which seeks to avoid the challenging and agonizing questions of the day. Rather, in Merton's own words, ". . . it embraces all the best hopes and intuitions of the modern world of science and technology, and unites them with the spiritual vision of Christianity."[20]

The power for peace in the great encyclical *Pacem in Terris* lies in its profoundly optimistic Christian spirit and in its radical belief in people. Pope John's vision lay in the belief that because man was made by God to seek peace and to achieve it, then no matter how confused people may be or become, the universal call to peace can be fulfilled. This uncompromising belief in the ultimate possibility of peace and unity was one of the greatest gifts that Pope John gave to Thomas Merton.

What was said at the time of the tenth anniversary of *Pacem in Terris* is still valid today. On that occasion Cardinal Roy wrote, "*Pacem in Terris* . . . retains all its originality: love and confidence in man, realistic optimism, and reading of the signs of the times, an unlimited dialogue and communion."[21]

The Christian Ethic of Nonviolence

Merton's approach to war and peace in the context of modern society constitutes a valid contemporary Christian ethic based upon the model established by Pope John XXIII. The way of nonviolence advocated by this very vocal monk can be seen as a coherent, far-reaching social ethic based upon the deepest of Christian motives and ideals. Although never a systematic writer, Merton used his writings as much as a means of expressing his ideas as discovering them almost out loud. From his unique perspective he addressed himself to the crucial ethical questions of his day and gradually developed his social ethic of nonviolence.

The role of the Christian philosopher, commentator, and ethicist is to ask questions of all people and of the world in the context of revealed truths. Merton did just that. These questions should then be evaluated, resolved, or answered in the light of the Gospel. Merton saw the philosophy of Christian nonviolence as the most effective way of responding to these social questions. His presentation was more of a way of life than a theory, more of an authentic life-style, involving the entire person, than an abstraction. It becomes, when taken in its deepest meaning and significance, a true philosophy of life, to be interiorized and put into practice in daily life.

This quality of honest questioning constitutes Merton as an authentic Christian thinker of our time. He constantly asked questions which attempted to find a meaning for contemporary existence, both for himself and for modern people. He once wrote: "I do not have clear answers to current questions. I do have questions, and, as a matter of fact, I think a man is known better by his questions than by his answers. To make known one's questions is, no doubt, to come out in the open oneself."[22]

Merton's thinking, like that of the Christian existentialist Gabriel Marcel, was not an impersonal abstract system, but a way of thinking and living that grew from personal reflection and experience. Rather than sitting back and impersonally contemplating the world, Merton, like Marcel, allowed himself to be struck *by* the world. But even more importantly, he allowed himself to react and respond to this lived experience. Thinking and writing is thus not seen as an optional game or a theoretical pursuit, but a necessity in order to clarify existence and make sense out of it. Such contemplation and reflection in the midst of the modern world is not "sterile, foolish and wasteful,"[23] as some accuse, but an indispensable need if we are to remain fruitful, sane, and peace-making Christians.

The social and political dimensions of this approach are manifold, for the awakening of the Christian conscience must be directed to the temporal and political spheres of life. First, however, it presupposes profound spiritual revolution and renewal, and Merton tried his best to make this revolution and renewal a reality.

Merton never ceased to remind Christians, especially American Christians, of their responsibility to work for peace and to find alternatives to war and violence for resolving national and international conflicts. He considered this problem an urgent one on the practical level, and one in which all Christians should be involved. "The Christian has a duty," he maintained, "as a Christian to contribute everything he can to help this great common work: of finding non-military and nonviolent ways of defending our rights, our interests, and our ideals."[24]

He rejoiced in the words of Pope John XXIII, who pointed out that Christians are obliged to strive for peace "with all the means at their disposal."[25] Merton took this theme and declared that all Christians are "bound to work for peace by working against global dissolution and anarchy . . . and must seek to build rather than destroy."[26]

In order to accomplish this, the poisonous effects of the mass media had to be overcome. The mass media constantly keep violence, cruelty, and sadism present to the minds of many impressionable people, especially youth. Merton realized that a falsely informed public, with a distorted view of political reality and an oversimplified, negative attitude toward other races and peoples, cannot be expected to react in any other way than with irrational and violent responses. The way of nonviolence would not come easily or without obstacles, but that should not deter Christians from making the necessary effort. "Ambiguity, hesitation and compromise are no longer possible. . . . The task of the Christian is to make the thought of peace once again seriously possible."[27]

This aspect of responsibility plays an important role in the ethic of nonviolence. "If we are disciples of Christ, we are necessarily our brother's keepers."[28] Here, as so often, Merton took the positive, direct approach emphasizing that not only is the Christian bound to avoid certain evils but is responsible for very great goods. He firmly believed that the doctrine of the Incarnation leaves the Christian obligated at once to God and to man. "If God has become man, then no Christian is ever allowed to be indifferent to man's fate."[29]

The impact of the Christian's responsibility is that he must not so much take one side or the other in the power struggles that exist but commit himself totally to God, to truth, and to the betterment of the whole of mankind. This global, supranational vision flows from Merton's openness to all peoples and ideas and is thoroughly catholic in the widest sense of the word.

In order to live out and practice this responsibility however, and to strive for peace and unity, dissent may, at times, be necessary, especially in the face of destructive social unjustices. While admitting a patriotic dissent, it must be responsible and used with great discretion. Merton warns against an ambiguous protest or dissent, merely to capture the attention of the press and gain publicity for a cause. This sometimes tends only to confuse people all the more and turn them against the cause which may be good in itself. Merton felt, for instance, that the public burning of draft cards and some of the public demonstrations against the Vietnam War caused more harm than good; although in the long run, he felt they accomplished a great deal.[30]

Part of the co-responsibility which Christians share with all others is the obligation to help one another. When this involves dissent, there are certain guidelines to be followed, for what is needed is a constructive, consistent, and clear dissent. A dissent that is both responsible and forceful ". . . recalls people to their senses, makes them think deeply, plants in them a seed of change, and awakens in them the profound need for truth, reason and peace which is implanted in man's nature."[31]

Such a responsible dissent implies a belief in openness of mind and in the possibility of a mature exchange of ideas. Merton insisted upon keeping an open mind toward the adversary or opponent. This genuine openness is a necessary prerequisite for any real dialogue which would lead to the resolution of a conflict or disagreement by nonviolent means. Without this openness and dialogue, the only recourse, at least the traditional one, is to weapons, force, or reprisals.

This openness, so characteristic of Merton, is an integral part of his nonviolent way. It is not naive or based upon a weak-willed or compromising approach but is firmly rooted "on that respect for the human person without which there is no deep and genuine Christianity."[32] It is primarily concerned with an appeal to the liberty and intelligence of the person, especially insofar as the person is able to transcend personal desires and national interests. This flows from Merton's Christian and optimistic view of man. Instead of forcing a decision upon someone from the outside, as many so-called "wars of liberation" purport to do, this view respects the integrity and freedom of the individual person.

A violent or coercive approach denies man's basic freedom and liberty in deciding his own future and destiny. Merton, on the other hand, invites man" . . . to arrive freely at a decision of his own, in dialogue and cooperation, and in the presence of that truth which Christian nonviolence brings into full view by its sacrificial witness."[33] This willingness to dialogue openly is an important insight into an indispensable aspect of a true philosophy of nonviolence. Taken even further we see that ". . . the key to nonviolence is the willingness of the nonviolent resister to suffer a certain amount of accidental evil in order to bring about a change of mind in the oppressor and awaken him to personal openness and to dialogue."[34]

Merton did not simply advocate openness for others, but he was ready to be open and willing to change his mind or stand corrected when the evidence indicated that he should. He tried to be responsive to new ideas and to listen to criticism. He has been described as ". . . a humble man who was always responsive to a new idea that might increase his awareness of life and understanding of reality . . . he always viewed himself as radically as possible, willing to change directions when he saw an error in his present way of thinking."[35]

True and False Nonviolence

Espousing the way of nonviolence is not without its difficulties and dangers. It must first of all not be considered as just a novel tactic or interesting method in trying to resolve conflict. Nor is it, Merton warns, simply a way of proving one's point and getting what a person wants "without being involved in behavior that one considers ugly and evil."[36]

Merton also warned against using nonviolence for purposes which were not good or worthy. He strongly felt that it would discredit and distort the truth of nonviolent resistance "to practice nonviolence for a purely selfish or arbitrary end."[37] It would likewise be an abuse of this tactic to use nonviolence merely in order to gain political advantage at the expense of the opponent's violent mistakes.

Practicing nonviolence for wrong or selfish motives must always be avoided. Nor should anyone have the attitude that he is virtuous or right and that his hands and heart are pure, while the adversary's may be evil and defiled. Care must be taken that nonviolence does not become a form of moral aggression, provoking in subtle ways, the evil that one hopes to find in an adversary.

Merton was concerned about a form of moral self-righteousness, and a "better-than-thou" attitude. True Christian nonviolence is built not on division, but on the basic unity among peoples. The aim of nonviolence is not so much the conversion of the wicked to the ideas of the good, "but for the healing and reconciliation of man with himself, man the person and man the human family."[38]

The nonviolent resister is not fighting simply for *his* truth or for *his* pure conscience, or for the right that is on *his* side. On the contrary, both his strength and his weakness come from the fact that he is fighting precisely for *the* truth which is common to both himself and the adversary.[39] The right which is both objective and universal is the aim of nonviolence. The nonviolent resister, the one who opposes injustice and untruth, is fighting for everyone.[40]

The "Evangelical realism" of the Gospels demands that the Christian cannot let himself be persuaded that the adversary is totally wicked and therefore can never be reasonable or well-intentioned. This attitude would defeat the very purpose of nonviolence—openness, communication, and dialogue.

The nonviolent Christian must do all he can to enter into dialogue with the adversary in order to attain the greater common good of all. At the same time, to be effective, nonviolence must be realistic and concrete. Like ordinary political action, nonviolence, "is no more than the 'art of the possible.' But precisely the advantage of nonviolence is that it lays claim to a more Christian and more humane notion of what is possible."[41]

This is one of the great advantages and also paradoxes of Christian nonviolence. While the powerful believe that only power is and can be efficacious, the nonviolent person is convinced of the superior efficacy of love, openness, peaceful negotioation, and, above all, of truth. "Power," Merton states, "can guarantee the interests of *some men* but, it can never foster the good of *man*. Power always protects the good of some at the expense of all the others."[42] Only love can attain and preserve the good of all, and this is what makes true nonviolence so thoroughly Christian.

This analysis of power is one of the keys in understanding the way of nonviolence as envisioned by Merton. He believed, on the one hand, that a true and valid nonviolence is a power and perhaps remains as the only really effective way of transforming man and human society. Here, however, as in many other areas, Merton is often vague and lacks in specifics. This weakness in his presentation, on the other hand, does enhance the dimension of universality that he considered so important. We can only view this lack of detail as a challenge to supply it in future formulations of nonviolence.

Conditions for Relative Honesty in the Practice of Christian Nonviolence

In his quest for truth and nonviolence, Merton did not exempt even himself from scrutiny and evaluation. Concerned about true and false nonviolence, he gave seven conditions for the honest practice of nonviolence which serve as characteristics of his way to peace.[43]

(1) Nonviolence must strike a balance between being too political and being totally apolitical. It must be aimed, above all, at the transformation of the present state of the world. It must be free from involvement in and with unjust and established power structures that abuse their authority. (2) The way of nonviolence is especially difficult for someone who belongs to one of the powerful nations. As an American, Merton knew the particular difficulties that were involved in being a privileged member of world society. He warned that nonviolence for such a person must not be for himself but for others, the poor and the underprivileged. In the case for the American Blacks, however, though they may be citizens of a privileged nation, their case is clearly different. They are entitled to wage a nonviolent struggle for their rights. But again, this struggle must be primarily for truth itself, as this will be their principal source of power.

(3) In the nonviolent struggle for peace, the threat of nuclear war abolishes all privileges. Nuclear weapons do not distinguish between rich and poor, in fact, the richest nations are the most threatened. On this point, a facile and fanatical self-righteousness must be avoided; self-justifying gestures should not be indulged. (4) To be a valid form of nonviolence, all desire—"fetishism," Merton terms it—must be avoided in the hope of obtaining immediate, visible results. One of the tasks of the nonviolent Christian is to restore a different standard of practical judgment in social conflict. This means nothing less than that the Christian humility of nonviolent action must establish itself in the minds and memories of modern people not only as conceivable and possible, but as a desirable alternative to what these people now consider the only realistic possibility—namely, political manipulation backed by force.

(5) The Christian practitioner of nonviolence must be convinced that the manner and method in which the conflict for truth is waged will itself manifest or obscure the truth. Here again, Merton prescribed limits to the fight for truth. Dishonest, violent, inhuman, or unreasonable means would simply betray the truth that one is trying to vindicate. "The absolute refusal of evil or suspect means is a necessary element in the witness of nonviolence."[44]

(6) Total openness to truth is a necessity. A test of one's sincerity in

the practice of nonviolence is the willingness to learn something from the adversary. It must be remembered that no enemy or antagonist is totally inhuman, wrong, unreasonable, or cruel. The readiness to see some good in an adversary, although tactically it may look like a weakness, actually gives power—the power of sincerity and truth. Nonviolence has great power provided it really witnesses to truth and not to self-righteousness.

(7) Christian hope is inseparable from Christian nonviolence. The quality of nonviolence is decided largely by the purity of the Christian hope behind it. Merton believed that the role of Christian humility in social life was to keep minds open to many diverse alternatives. It is important to understand that Christian humility implies not only a certain wise reserve in regard to one's own judgments, but it also anticipates positive and trustful expectations of others. It is not a false, self-pitying humility, but a positive humility of openness to others. This humility of nonviolence is nothing less than the meekness and humbleness of heart which Christ extolled in the Sermon on the Mount. It is the basis of true Christian nonviolence.

In keeping with Merton's conditions for honesty in the practice of nonviolence, Francis X. Meehan warns that while one must work nonviolently in every issue, one "must be willing to undergo some nonsuccess—even some misunderstanding."[45]He goes on to say that we must guard aginst a "passivity satisfied with the status quo. . . . We have to realize that it may be a somewhat comfortable North American affluence that allows us to speak *easily* in behalf of nonviolence."[46]

Thus it is seen that while it is difficult to practice nonviolence, and one must be kept constantly vigilant and honest, it is nonetheless possible and desirable. Merton gives a few examples of people who have tried to live the way of nonviolence, and in some cases to die for it.

Some Who Have Tried

Merton lauds the attempts of certain people to live the way of nonviolent resistance to evil and injustice, even while their approach may in some ways differ from his own. Besides the classic example of Gandhi, whom we have already discussed, Merton frequently cited the Austrian peasant Franz Jägerstätter. Declared an "enemy of the state" by the German military authorities, Jägerstätter was beheaded in 1943. His crime was his refusal to fight in what he considered an unjust war and repeatedly refusing to take the military oath.

His objection to military service was the fruit of his own reflection and religious interpretation of contemporary political events. While the Church was officially going along with Hitler, and his friends, relatives, priests, and bishops all encouraged him to take up arms, Jägerstätter felt that spiritual weapons, especially prayer, were needed more.[47]

Merton compares his decision of heroic self-sacrifice to that of Thomas More and does not hesitate to call Jägerstätter a martyr. He is, in many ways, a precursor of the current view of the Catholic Church on the right to conscientious objection.[48]

Another example of a conscientious objector during World War II was Dietrich Bonhoeffer. Bonhoeffer took a firm stand against Hitler and his godlessness at a time when other Christians marched with Hitler in his violence against humanity. Bonhoeffer was "absolutely opposed to Nazism and to all that it stood for."[49] Bonhoeffer's resistance against Hitlerism was dictated by his Christian conscience, and as a result he spent two years in prison for his conscientious objection. He was finally hung on April 9, 1945, seeking God to the end and protesting against Nazi godlessness, while so many of the "religious" lined up behind Hitler's armies and marched in the godless military parade.[50]

A man who discovered in the solitude and emptiness and desperation of imprisonment the truth of what is entailed in the quest for inner peace was Fr. Alfred Delp. A Jesuit, he was condemned to be executed as a traitor to Nazi Germany for advocating true Christian humanism. In his challenging personal meditation written in prison, Fr. Delp asked some basic questions of himself, his Church, and the world.[51] He confronts modern man in much the same way as Merton does, with the challenge to set about the difficult work of restoring order to society and bringing peace to the world, starting with individual personal witness. Merton rejoiced at his impassioned plea for Christian liberty and personal dignity in the midst of the degradation of prison and war.

Fr. Delp diagnosed the moral climate of the world as a sickness of passive people, too uncommitted to the truth to resist the lies of war and social injustice. Merton saw in this man a living example of one who, by his very life, embodied the way of nonviolent resistance to evil and suffering and shared it with others.

In an essay entitled, "A Martyr for Peace and Unity,"[52] Merton discussed the example of Max Josef Metzger, a Catholic priest executed by Hitler's Gestapo in Berlin in 1944. A true patriot, Fr. Metzger was a devoted worker in the cause of peace. In his letters protesting against the abuse of power by Hitler, he wrote that "it is honorable to die for one's country, but still more honorable to die for righteousness and peace."[53]

Agreeing with the basic thought of Fr. Metzger, Merton gave some of his own reflections on the position of the Christian committed to the practice of nonviolence in the midst of a nation committed to war. The position of Metzger in wartime Germany was similar to that of Merton in the United States during the Vietnam conflict. Merton wrote: ". . . Let us remember this formula: in the madness of modern war, when every crime is justified, the nation is always right, power is always right, the military is always right. To question those who wield power, to differ from then in any way, is to confess oneself subversive, rebellious, traitors. Fr. Metzger did not believe in power, in bombs. He believed in Christ, in unity, in peace. He died as a martyr for his belief."[54]

One of the qualities Merton most admired in Simone Weil, the French writer and philosopher, was her personal vocation to absolute intellectual honesty. She was associated with pacifism as far back as the 1930s, and her passion for integrity and abhorrence of violence led her to see a core of a metaphysics in nonviolence.[55]

Simone Weil wrote an article in 1937 which Merton considered one of the classic treatments of the problem of war and peace in our time. "The acceptance of war," she wrote, "as an unavoidable fatality is the root of the power politician's ruthless and obsessive commitment to violence."[56]

Weil refers to collective power, and the urge to collective power, as the "great beast" which seeks to control and eventually devour those whom it is supposed to serve. As a leader of the French resistance movement during World War II, she saw the abuses of collective power running rampant through Europe. In order to combat these abuses she advocated nonviolence, but a nonviolence that is truly effective because it is strong. Merton noted that ineffective nonviolence is the nonviolence of the weak. It merely submits to evil without real resistance. Effective nonviolence, on the other hand, is the nonviolence of the strong. It opposes evil with a serious and positive resistance in trying to overcome it with good.[57]

Merton lamented the fact that the nonviolent resistance of Simone Weil was never fully developed. But her hope that some day someone might substitute more nonviolence in the place of violence has not fallen on deaf ears. She died in 1943, refusing to eat anything more than what was given to her compatriots in occupied France, resisting in a nonviolent way the horror of war.

These few examples, very briefly presented in capsule form, were used by Merton to demonstrate the effectiveness that nonviolent resistance can have and the ways in which it could be practiced. Through the example of their own lives, each in their own way gave concrete, personal witness to the way of nonviolence as a viable alternative to violence and as a protest against war and injustice. Another example of someone who lived and preached nonviolence that Merton greatly respected, Martin Luther King, will be discussed in the next chapter which deals with racism and violence.

Chapter V
Racism and Violence

The two social issues which Thomas Merton considered most urgent to Americans during the 1960s were war and racism. He applied his ethic of nonviolence to both these pressing social problems along with his insightful analysis. He had long been aware of the tragedy of the racial situation in the United States. As far back as the 1930s he saw the potential explosiveness of the Black ghettoes, which he said were clearly the creation of the dominant white society.[1]

Twenty years ahead of the times, Merton realized that the Black people were hostile to white society and culture. He was certain that there was ". . . not a Negro in the whole place (Harlem) who can fail to know, in the marrow of his bones that the white man's culture is not worth the jetsam in the Harlem River."[2]

Merton himself worked in Harlem for a short time, where he joined Catherine de Hueck, foundress of Friendship House. One of his earliest commentaries on the dangers of segregating the worlds of Black and white America was a poem written in the 1950s and dedicated to Baroness de Hueck. A poem of keen social protest, it vividly describes Merton's insight into the conditions that led to racial revolution twenty years later. The poem reads:

> Across the cages of the keyless aviaries,
> The lines and wires, the gallows of the broken kites,
> Crucify, against the fearful light,
> The rugged dresses of the little children.

Soon, in the sterile jungles of the waterpipes
    and ladders,
The bleeding sun, a bird of prey, will terrify the poor,
Who will forget the unbelievable moon. . .
The white men's wives, like Pilate's,
Cry in the peril of their frozen dreams:
"Daylight has driven iron spikes,
into the flesh of Jesus' hands and feet:
Four flowers of blood have nailed Him to the walls
    of Harlem."[3]

Merton's sensitive description of Harlem in *The Seven Storey Mountain* so impressed Eldridge Cleaver, the Black spokesman and author, that he copied it out in longhand and kept it with him at all times. Cleaver recounts in one of his own books that he would refer to these notes when giving Black Muslim lectures.[4]

The terrible racial crisis which exploded in the United States in the 1960s was the inevitable coming to a head of a long, immoral subjection of the Black people by the whites. In the early days of the Civil Rights Movement the Black man thought that the white man could be trusted. But after the enactment of the Civil Rights Bill in 1964, with no subsequent action or implementation following from it, the Black man gradually became more frustrated and inclined to violence. At that point it ceased to be a 'movement'' and became a "revolution."[5]

Baker accurately observes about Merton that throughout his career ". . . from the early responses to Harlem through the discussion of Gandhi and Martin Luther King to his late poetry of universal scope, Merton consistently and insistently blamed the racial crisis in America on the white man."[6]

Merton discussed the tendency on the part of the white man in every age and all over the world to make slaves of darker races. White men have permitted darker peoples to have an identity only if it corresponded with their own concept of them as darker and inferior people. In keeping with his emphasis on personal identity, Merton wrote that the ultimate violence which one man can do to another is to impose upon him an invented identity. This in turn puts him into a position of servitude and helplessness in which he finally accepts the imposed identity as substantially true. Merton charged that this is what white men have done around the world, including the United States.[7]

The White Liberal's Sin

Aside from several articles and reviews, Merton's main writing on racism is contained in two books. The first is *The Seeds of Destruction*, written during 1963–64. In Part One, entitled "Black Revolution," Merton wrote several "Letters to a White Liberal." In these letters he asserted that the white liberal was largely responsible for the racial conflict in the United States.[8]

Most white liberals, he contended, were basically ignorant of the racial situation, of the Black man's true motives and feelings. Although he might be well-meaning, the average white liberal would sell the Black man down the river in order to protect himself. Thus, many liberals get involved in roles of leadership in the Civil Rights Movement not so much to help the Black people attain their full stature as persons and citizens, but to control their fight for rights. In this way white liberals can apply the brakes when they feel it is necessary.[9]

White liberals really confused the racial situation by giving the impression that Blacks have a place in white society, when the majority do not want or accept Blacks. Merton actually felt that the presence of white people at the famous march on Washington in 1963 hurt the cause of the Blacks since it created the illusion that the Black man had a place waiting for him in white America. Since the purpose of the Washington march was to demonstrate that the Black is an outcast from American society, white liberals actually distorted its whole meaning and made the issue ambiguous.[10]

Merton believed that all hope for really constructive and positive results in the Civil Rights Movement should be placed squarely in the hands of the Christian, nonviolent Black leaders. But, at the same time, he expressed his fear that leaders, such as Martin Luther King, would lose their power when more Blacks realized that the majority of white Americans in spite of the Civil Rights Bill had no intention of allowing them a role in society. Merton feared that the courageous struggle of moderate leaders, dedicated to nonviolence, would give way to proponents of violence and destruction. His fears in 1964, unfortunately, proved to be true. The mid-1960s witnessed the sad race riots and burning of homes in many American cities, under the leadership of the Black Muslims and Black Panther groups.

Merton chided white Americans and especially white liberals. He stated that where minds are full of hatred, and imaginations dwell on cruelty, torment, punishment, and revenge, inevitably violence and death will follow. The problem as he saw it was that if the Black man was to enter wholly into white society, "then that society is going to be radically changed."[11] This would be very demanding on the part of the white man psychologically, emotionally, and financially. Today, Merton shouted, is the time to acknowledge it and prepare for it. "We must dare to pay the dolorous price of change," he said, "to grow into a new society. Nothing else will suffice."[12]

From the sociological point of view, Merton's analysis of the racial situation in 1964 was not remarkably original, but his sense of urgency and foresight were incisive. He called upon all Americans, and white Christians, in particular to accept the difficulties and sacrifices involved in order to achieve an integrated society. Christianity is concerned with human crises, and Christians are called to manifest the mercy and truth of God in history. Surely the crisis and the time had come.

Kairos: Hope of Unity

The irony of the Civil Rights Movement was the fact that the hour of freedom for the Black people would also be the hour of freedom for the white people. The radical situation, as Merton saw it, was a *kairos,* a providential hour.[13] The Black man was offering the white man a "message of salvation," an occasion to enter with him into a providential reciprocity willed by God. He was issuing an invitation for the white man to understand him as necessary for his own life, and as completing it. The Blacks were asking the whites to listen and pay some attention to what they had to say. The Black people seriously demanded that the white people learn something from them.

Merton warned the white man, blinded by his self-conceit and his illusion of self-sufficiency, that if he failed to heed the Black man's call, the Black man would cease to call and begin to burn and shoot.

Quite simply, Merton maintained that white society has sinned through injustices and cruelties to the Black man, sometimes unconsciously, but sometimes with malice of forethought. "The time has come," he wrote, ". . . when both white and Black have been granted by God, a unique and momentous opportunity to repair this injustice and to re-establish the violated moral and social order on a new plane."[14]

In keeping with his Christian interpretation of history, Merton advocated that the sin of the white man be expiated through a genuine response to the Black man. This atonement should consist of two things: (1) a complete reform of the social system which permits and breeds such injustices; (2) this work of reorganization must be carried out under the inspiration of the Black man whose providential time has now arrived. At this point in history the Black man has received from God enough light, ardor, and spiritual strength to free the white man in freeing himself from the white man.[15]

Merton completely endorsed leaders such as Martin Luther King, Jr., who based his struggle upon the nonviolent philosophy of Gandhi. Such leadership accepted suffering, not only to gain freedom for the Black man but also to save the white man's soul by showing him his sin of injustice.[16]

Merton was pleased that the students and people involved in the Civil Rights Movement were convinced of nonviolence as their basic approach. This is borne out in such preambles as the "Statement of Purpose" adopted at the Atlanta, Georgia, meeting of the Student Nonviolent Coordinating Committee. The Statement, drawn up in 1966, said in part: "We affirm the philosophy or religious ideal of non-violence as the fundamental of our purpose. The presupposition of our faith and the manner of our action, nonviolence as it grows from the Judaeo-Christian traditions, seeks a social order of justice permeated by love."[17]

The Civil Rights Movement was a real social issue in which the practice of the nonviolent way could bring about effective change and new attitudes. The white man, however, must respond to the *kairos* of the situation—or be damned. Christians, Black and white alike, must recall that they have been liberated and redeemed by an inner truth that should make them obey and listen to the Lord of History.

Merton often wrote in eschatological terms, stating that the survival of America was itself in question. He felt that the followers of Dr. Martin Luther King believed that the sin of white America had reached such a proportion that it might call down a dreadful judgment, "perhaps total destruction on the whole country, unless atonement is made."[18]

As in his analysis of nonviolence and war, Merton viewed the purpose of nonviolent protest and action in its deepest and most spiritual dimensions ". . . to awaken the conscience of the white man to the awful reality of his injustice and his sin, so that he will be able to see that the Negro problem is really a white problem: that the cancer of injustice and hate which is eating white society and is only partly manifested in racial segregation with all its consequences, *is rooted in the heart of the white man himself.*"[19]

White Society

The racial situation gave rise to some of Merton's most trenchant criticisms of American society. Black nonviolence as a radical challenge and source of uneasiness and fear, forced white society to admit that its prosperity was rooted, to some extent, in injustice and sin.

Questioning America's right to claim to be the only sincere defenders of the human person, of his rights, and of his dignity, Merton felt that

America had little genuine interest in human liberty and in the human person. The plight of the American black people was a prime example.

Americans, on the contrary, were more interested in the unlimited freedom of the corporation. Himself included, Merton said that when Americans talk about the "free world," they mean first of all the world in which business is free. The freedom of of the person comes after that, and is dependent upon money. Without money, freedom would have no meaning. "And therefore the most basic freedom of all is the freedom to make money."[20] In other words, we are not so much interested in persons as profits. American society is organized first and foremost with a view to business: profit first, people afterward.

The Civil Rights Movement and the Black demonstrations were taken seriously only when they began to hurt business. It is not the life of the spirit that is real to most Americans, but the vitality of the market.

One of the major reasons why Merton viewed the racial conflict as a *kairos*, was that it afforded American society a chance for self-examination and self-evaluation. He believed that the entire Western culture of the United States and Europe was at stake, and that Western man must free himself from the tyranny of materialism and big business. The Black man was affording him the opportunity to do this. As we have already seen with regard to war, Merton believed that a permanent solution of the race problem was only possible if there was a widespread change, a real *metanoia*, within people's hearts. This is one of the great challenges Merton issued to modern, contemporary society, as true today as when he first issued it.

Merton thought one of the best expressions of the concept of *kairos* was in the novel *A Different Drummer* by William Melvin Kelly. It was a symbolic statement on the part of the Black people; it was a final rejection of the paternalism and servitude imposed upon them by a white society. It was the announcement that the hour of the Black man's destiny had arrived. It was a final and definite "No" to the white American's social order and cultural system.[21]

The Black novelist and essayist James Baldwin ranked with Martin

Luther King as one of the most influential Black spokesmen according to Merton. His novel *Go Tell It on the Mountain* had much to say about the motives and spirit of the Black Revolution in America.[22]

Martin Luther King did more than anyone through his writings and example to inspire the Civil Rights Movement with the spirit of Christian nonviolence. Merton never tired of praising King and encouraging white Americans to read and to ponder his words.[23]

Martin Luther King, the central figure in the Southern Christian Leadership Conference, used techniques of nonviolence and of the Gandhian spirit in his search for relevant strategy in the struggle against racism. He himself fell victim to the violence he so abhorred. He was assassinated in 1968 believing to the end in the necessity and power of nonviolence in bringing about effective and lasting social change.

From Nonviolence to Black Power

The second major book in which Merton discussed racism was *Faith and Violence*, published in 1968, after the previous summer's race riots and widespread violence across the United States. Merton largely attributed the transition from nonviolence to violent Black Power to the fact that integration was won on the law books but was lost in fact. The result was that nonviolence both ''as a tactic and as a mystique has been largely rejected as irrelevant by the American Negro.''[24]

Most Black Americans came to view the Black Power movement in the United States as more effective and more meaningful than Christian nonviolence. This failure of nonviolence to bring about social change demonstrated, according to Merton, the stark reality that American society was radically violent and that violence was built into its very structure.

The Vietnam war, Merton felt, had a great deal to do with the trend toward violence and Black Power. The Vietnam war was viewed by many as yet another manifestation of the white man's versatility in beating down non-whites. An America that destroyed Vietnamese non-combatants with napalm has no right to object when Blacks at home burn down their slums or protest violently against real injustices.

Merton agreed with Black leader H. Rap Brown who said that violence was thoroughly American, in fact, was the real American language. Merton recognized that there was a great deal of truth to the accusation of white America in Brown's statement: "Violence is part of your culture."[25]

In Merton's assessment, the Black Power movement was directed specifically against the white liberals and their ambiguous consciences. The Black Power movement was not just racism in reverse, but had to appear racist; (1) to help the Black man consolidate his sense of identity; (2) to rebuff the sentimental and meddling integrationism of the white liberal; and (3) to get the liberals off the Black man's back, and to make it quite clear that the black man wanted to run his own liberation movement.[26]

The real thrust of the Black Power movement was toward the acquisition of a political power that would ensure real influence and a serious ability to participate in the economic life of the country on equal terms with white people. This legitimate and just aim was misrepresented by the white mass media and white society in general.

The Black Power movement was, in the opinion, of many identified with and involved in the global revolutionary ferment in the Third World—the liberation of oppressed people across the world. The Black Power movement was seen as part of a ". . . world movement of refusal and rejection of the value system we call Western culture. It is therefore at least implicitly critical of Christianity as white man's religion."[27]

The Task of the Christian

Merton stated quite emphatically that he believed that the Christian was obligated, by his commitment to Christ, "to seek out effective and authentic ways of peace in the midst of violence."[28] Merely demanding support and obedience to an established "disorder" which is essentially violent, did not qualify he said, as authentic "peace-making."

The only real solution, as Merton saw it, was to deal with the evil root of violence—the hatred, poison, cruelty and greed which are part of the system itself. The task of the white Christian was ". . . partly a job of diagnosis and criticism, a prophetic task of finding and identifying the injustice which is the cause of *all* the violence, both white and Black, which is also the root of war, and of the greed which keeps war going in order that some might make money out of it."[29]

Merton was fully cognizant that neither he nor any Christian had facile answers to such social problems. He advocated that the task of the Christian was to struggle along with the Black man in the difficult and frustrating task of seeking a solution to common problems. In this way the American racial crisis would offer the American Christian a chance to recover his fidelity to Christian truth and not to perpetuate the Christian failure in American racial justice. This failure, Merton contended, was largely due to the fact that ". . . so few Christians have been able to face the fact that nonviolence comes very close to the heart of the Gospel ethic, and is perhaps essential to it."[30]

The Spiral of Violence

Dom Helder Camara, Archbishop of Olinda and Recife in the underdeveloped Northeast of Brazil, although using different terminology, has many points of similarity with Merton's analysis of violence in society. Dom Helder writes that the basic form of violence, which he calls Violence No. 1, is injustice. This form of violence in society, does not necessarily do direct physical harm, but is a "violation of personhood."[31] Like Merton, Dom Helder sees this structural violence as a subtle, institutionalized destruction of human possibilities.

When the injustice of society becomes too oppressive, Violence No. 2, which Dom Helder calls revolt, bursts forth. Like Merton's view of the 1967 race riots in the United States, Helder Camara maintains that violence as revolt takes place when injustice has reached the place where a large group of people will no longer bear it passively or silently.[32]

Just as Violence No. 1 (injustice) leads to Violence No. 2(revolt), so does Violence No. 2 lead to Violence No. 3, which Dom Helder terms repression. Confronted with revolt, those who hold power put down the revolt by whatever repressive means are necessary to ensure that their power is not threatened. Camara is in accord with Merton in the belief that violence attracts violence and is followed by repression. The presence of the National Guard and police dogs during the race riots of 1968 is an example of this. Merton compared that situation to a Nazi police state.[33]

Unlike other revolutionaries in South America, however, Helder Camara does not advocate violence but calls for radical nonviolence to effect social change. One biographer of Camara describes him in a fashion that Merton himself has often been characterized, ". . . a man of peace, forced to live in a world of conflict and violence. For him, the way of peace is not a mere political tactic: it is a way of life."[34]

Dom Helder Camara was a featured speaker in Philadelphia during the 41st International Eucharistic Congress, held in August 1976. His constant plea, which received a great deal of media attention, was for a nonviolent solution to the injustices in society. He denounced the "internal colonialism" in South America, where the rich hold onto their wealth, thereby forcing millions to live in a subhuman condition."[35]

Like Merton, Camara was very critical of "structural injustices" in society and constantly calls for the creation of a more human world open to the needs of all peoples. Camara espouses in the 1980s the same nonviolent alternatives to war and violence that Merton advocated in the late 1960s. Camara has called for the need to discover "new and different ways to fight communism . . . we must not fight a bad situation with another bad situation."[36]

Dom Helder Camara was the recipient of the Martin Luther King prize in 1975, for his work in the field of social justice. Like Merton, he urged a personal conversion and interior change of heart as the necessary beginning for any really effective change in the structure of society. Again, echoing the sentiments of Merton, Dom Helder wrote: "I accuse the real authors of violence: all those who, whether on the right or on the left, weaken true justice and prevent lasting peace. For me, my own personal vocation is that of a pilgrim of peace, following the example of Paul VI; personally I would prefer a thousand times to be killed than to kill."[37]

The Philosophy of Nonviolence

Merton did not hesitate to put forth his own solution to the race issue and all issues involving violence—Christian nonviolence. He saw nonviolence *not* as a way of avoiding conflict (as it is frequently caricatured) but as a particular technique and positive force for dealing with conflict. It proceeds from a conviction that violence is both morally evil and tactically counterproductive. It stems from the belief that nonviolence is both morally correct and pragmatically effective in the long run and the only really Christian solution.

Although Merton died before he was able to delineate more specifically the ways the philosophy of nonviolence would help to solve the racial crisis, he did stress the characteristics of nonviolence as given in the previous chapter. These elements agree substantially with the strategy of nonviolence advocated by Martin Luther King. Dr. King considered at least six points as pivotal for an understanding of the nonviolent position:

(1) Nonviolence is for the strong rather than the weak. It is a demanding discipline; it is not non-resistance but a particular method of resistance.

(2) Nonviolence does not seek to "defeat or humiliate" the opponent, but to win him over.

(3) Nonviolence directs itself "against the forces of evil rather than against persons who happen to be doing evil."

(4) Without making suffering into something to be sought, nonviolence can bring home the truth that "unearned suffering is redemptive."

(5) The attitude of nonviolence must be within the heart of the individual as well as in his outer actions.

(6) Nonviolence is "based on the conviction that the universe is on the side of justice. The practitioner can believe that he is not going against the grain of what is ultimate, but seeks rather to exemplify what is ultimate: redemptive suffering love."[38]

Toward Union and Reconciliation

Merton may be lacking in specifics and details, but he was quite certain of the long-range goal—union. He believed this to be the central teaching of Christianity—union of God with man, of religion with religion, and of man with man. All of his social commentary had this same unitive thrust.

Thus the ideal of Christian nonviolence in the racial crisis was to unify black with white. The man who espoused this ideal, instead of giving up in the face of increasing violence, should increase his efforts and strive with more determination to attain change through peaceful means. Merton's concern as a Christian monk was to repair the disunity which existed in the world and help heal the wounds of violence and division. There was only one way of accomplishing this task: ". . . the only philosophy and method which he believed capable of restoring unity to American and world affairs . . . was the Christian philosophy of nonviolent protest against injustice and war."[39]

Just as Merton's decision to enter a monastery in the early 1940s was a nonviolent protest against the chaos and disunity of man's society, so the mature monk of the 1960s felt justified and compelled in recommending the Christian philosophy of nonviolence to all people of good will.

A major obstacle, Merton was convinced, was that the common

image of nonviolence in the minds of most Americans was "largely negative and completely inadequate."[40] Many Americans embraced a myth which regarded nonviolence which appeals directly to the Gospels, as basically unChristian and ineffective. Reliance on force and cooperation in massive programs of violence and defense were often seen, however, as essential and as an unquestionable duty.

Merton sought to make the American public aware of the fact that nonviolence, rather than attacking the ideals of Christianity or of democratic society, was the fulfillment and implementation of these ideals. He constantly reiterated the positive values of nonviolence and stressed its compatibility with the Gospel ethic. He viewed it as a practical, descriptive philosophy upon which a modern Christian could build a program of social action.[41] He presented the challenge of Christian nonviolence as a way of approaching and resolving the explosive issue of racism in America. This is an issue which is still with us today and needs the nonviolent way more than ever. After almost two decades since Merton said it was time to begin, the *kairos* has long since come, his challenge is not to miss this *kairos,* fail to redeem it, or attempt to destroy it.

The nonviolence which Merton advocated was essentially a positive, constructive endeavor which presupposed that the conditions of society can be improved. Nonviolence strives to make the enemy—be he white or Black, soldier or civilian—an object of love, thereby liberating both the oppressor and the oppressed.

If nonviolence failed, and many Black people involved in the Civil Rights Movement believed that it had, Merton felt it was due not so much to an inherent weakness in the way of nonviolence but due rather to a society whose only language seemed to be that of violence. For nonviolence and moral pressure to be a real alternative to armed revolution, it is essential that the established regime should have a minimum of respect for the rights of man and especially freedom of expression. Merton was fearful that such a moral climate was fast disappearing in the United States and was determined to do all he could to reestablish and strengthen it.

Simplification ana Prophecy

As with much of his social criticism, Merton tended to oversimplify the racial crisis. He very narrowly placed the burden of racial strife on the white liberals' shoulders, calling it their sin. He often cited only those facts which supported his own theories and glossed over many of the more complex aspects of the racial problem.

His oversimplification, however, was not without design or effect. He often directed his simplified criticism against groups with which he himself was identified: he was white, an American, and a liberal. He thus pointed out the "sins" and faults of people with whom he himself was associated. His sometimes simplistic criticism of Americans and white liberals, in particular, was an example of his effective use of deliberate oversimplification. He succeeded in pointing out some real faults in American life with a forcefulness and impact that only a clear, concise, and simple approach could achieve.

Martin Marty, the Protestant theologian, in reviewing *The Seeds of Destruction* (1963) said that Merton had oversimplified and overstated the dangers of the white liberal and was unjustifiably pessimistic. Several years later, however, in an open letter to Merton, Marty apologized and admitted that Merton's predictions were coming true. Marty ended up applauding Merton's wisdom and perception and asked for constructive suggestions and roles which the white liberal might pursue.[42]

Merton characteristically replied that the white liberal should work behind the scenes, desiring no recognition or thanks. The white liberal of the future, in order to prove his sincerity, would be required to give nothing less than a Christian nonviolent response to violence.

In what Baker calls Merton's last will and testament to a racist America of the 1960s, Merton preached: "There is no white and Black in Christ . . . Black Power or no Black Power, I for one remain for the Negro. I trust him, I recognize the overwhelming justice of his complaint . . . as a Christian I owe him support, not in his ranks but in my own among the whites who refuse to trust him or hear him, and who want to destroy him."[43]

Merton had great foresight about the causes, nature, and development of the Civil Rights upheaval of the 1960s; his seeming pessimism was ultimately vindicated as realism. "He stood on the cutting edge of history, understanding and correctly interpreting recent developments and looking into the future to prophesy about coming events."[44]

As one of the foremost thinkers and writers to see the relationship between the war in Vietnam and the racial disturbances in America, Merton opposed both with equal vigor and zeal. He proposed the way of nonviolence as the only sane and Christian avenue to resolve these violent social questions. He never waivered from his conviction of the value of nonviolence as an effective form of protest and affirmation. But nonviolence is effective only when those who employ it have achieved the inner unity they seek to establish in society. Only when they have healed their own internal divisions, a healing which is the fruit of contemplation, can they build a unified social structure, the fruit of nonviolence where all peoples can live in peace and harmony.

Conclusion

In 1965 Winthrop Hudson wrote that Thomas Merton, along with Fulton J. Sheen, was a major symbol "of the post-World War II religious revival among Roman Catholics."[1]

Twelve years later, in 1977, Elena Malits wrote that Merton is ". . . a symbol and synthesis of contemporary Catholicism insofar as his life story embodies the profound transformation of attitudes and orientation we have experienced in recent years."[2] In 1981 we read that "scholars in the field of American religion have begun to notice a significant 'Merton phase' in the religious pilgrimage of many young people. No one has the slightest idea where it will all end—if indeed it ever does."[3]

Merton is indeed a man for our times, a voice in the wilderness that will lead us into the future. He is a seminal and perennial thinker and a commentator upon contemporary social issues. A man very much a part of and yet far ahead of his own time, Merton's message and challenge confronts society as much today as when he was writing in the late 1960s. Like a prophetic voice, often misunderstood and frequently ignored, his social thought and plea for nonviolence are only recently receiving the analysis, study, and public attention they rightly deserve.

Merton has been called "a man of Renaissance dimensions,"[4] and has been compared to Ralph Waldo Emerson.[5] His great versatility makes him "a kinsman to so many kinds of people . . . . and a brother to all who search for truth. He symbolizes and epitomizes modern man, head in the clouds, feet in quicksand, fighting every battle up hill but with a look of confidence on his face. .''[6]

This attempt to develope and analyze Merton's social thought has emphasized his social dimension of contemplation and Christian philosophy of nonviolence. As we have seen, the underlying theme of Merton's life has been his search for unity. His life was one of continual development, with each new stage building upon the others in a constant state of dynamic and dialectic tension. Throughout these various stages, Merton's consistent motivating force and drive was his quest for inner unity, the real source of nonviolence.

Although Merton was not a systematic thinker or writer, his thought developed and grew as he matured. He can rightly be called a journalistic philosopher. By this is meant one who writes a running commentary and critique of society from his own unique perspective and point of view—not systematically but as things happen, as they hit him. For these reasons Merton's writings are essentially autobiographical, since they reveal so much about the man himself, his feelings, and his beliefs. And, most assuredly, as any good commentator must, he expressed his opinions and interpreted current events.

Contemplation for Merton was an awakening, and an enlightenment. He had an awareness of questions and faced questions honestly. He once wrote, ''The question is, itself, the answer. And we ourselves are both.''[7] This increasing awareness and self-questioning are among Merton's greatest contributions. These aspects give his writings a certain timelessness and a validity twenty years later.

A true Mertonian question goes to the heart of the matter as it cuts through the facade of the empirical self and the sophistication of a scientific mind. Merton wanted modern man to confront himself on the deepest levels of being about the morality of social issues and the really important social questions of the day. To do anything less he felt was not only unchristian but irresponsible. His impassioned plea today is being heard loudly and clearly. The American Bishops are wrestling with many of these complex problems and are making a sincere and courageous effort to address them. Their pastural letter, *The Challenge of Peace: God's Promise and Our Response,* issued in May, 1983 honestly confronts the basic questions of war and peace in the nuclear age.

Merton viewed life as a constant search for God and a quest for inner unity. To attain unity and to discover one's God should be the task of all Christians. Merton's social commentary was the fruit of his quest for the Divine and his intense life of contemplation and solitude.

Merton's view was truly catholic, reaching out to all peoples and all religions. Like Teilhard de Chardin, the French Jesuit paleontologist, Merton sought to find all that was most human and most Christian in all peoples and in every part of the world. Like Teilhard, Merton was a mystic and poet, a prolific writer, and a controversial and contemporary religious figure.Merton, like Teilhard was also misunderstood by those within the Church, censored by his superiors, ahead of his time both personally and ideologically, but ultimately vindicated by his posthumous publications and subsequent analysis of his writings.

What Merton wrote about Teilhard can well be applied to himself; "(he had) a profound sympathy for everything human and for every legitimate aspiration of modern man, even though that man may sometimes be a misguided and errant thinker, a heretic, an atheist."[8] Just as Teilhard before him, Merton turned to the East and found there many of the aspirations of Christians and especially contemplatives. While remaining fully committed to Christianity and avoiding a false syncretism, Merton felt that he had a great deal to learn from Zen and the other great religions of the East. As a means to a transcultural and transformed consciousness, Merton saw Zen as a valuable way for modern Christians to come to a greater appreciation of themselves as well as attain greater unity with others and the world around them.

His concept of final integration and of the finally integrated person is the fulfillment of his basic thrust toward inner unity. One who practices contemplation, engages in the social action which flows from it, and seeks to make nonviolence a way of life, becomes similar to Merton's concept of the integrated personality. Merton was always concerned with self-identity and the quest for true self. Toward the end of his life, he wrote: "My task is only to be what I am, a man seeking God in silence and solitude, with deep respect for the demands and realities of his own vocation, and fully aware that others too are seeking the truth in their own way."[9] The fully integrated person is aware of and accepts himself and has a transcultural perspective and a sharply awakened consciousness. Thus the integrated person becomes a true peacemaker, capable of "making peace" because he has already achieved inner peace. It is the achievement of inner peace and the desire to create more peace that is the ultimate goal and objective of all contemplation and nonviolence. It was toward this goal that Merton dedicated the last years of his life and final writings.

The finally integrated person is the personification of the person of peace. As one who can transcend the complexities of modern society and yet be fully a part of that society, as one who is not duped by the mass media and yet is totally informed on key issues, the finally integrated person of peace has discovered his own inner being and unity through solitude and yet is at one with all people.

It is up to us as Christians to accept the challenge to follow the Gospel imperatives and at the same time strive to follow the way of nonviolence as modern peacemakers. Merton developed his philosophy of nonviolence as a countermeasure to the evils of war and violence which so afflict contemporary society. He proposed the way of nonviolence as a Christian, human, and peaceful alternative to war and conflict.

Whether criticizing the so-called "just war" theories or showing their inadequacy in the light of nuclear warfare, or quoting the early Church Fathers, Merton always looked for elements that would help his developing theory of nonviolence. As we have seen two of the pillars upon which Merton built his theory were Gandhi and Pope John XXIII. Gandhi's classic formulation of nonviolence and Pope John XXIII's *Pacem in Terris* provided Merton with many aspects and ideas which he integrated into his synthesis of nonviolence.

Always quick to point out the social obligations regarding attitudes toward war and the active pursuit of peace, Merton stressed the capacity to question oneself and the willingness to change and be open to others and opposing points of view. He was careful to distinguish between true and false ways of nonviolence, and always called for honesty in the practice of nonviolence. He was realistic about the dangers and misconceptions of a nonviolence that was to be a radical way of life. Undaunted, however, he strongly advocated the way of nonviolence as the true force of peace for the future.

Blessed are the Peacemakers

In concluding this study of Thomas Merton's quest for unity and nonviolence, we shall discuss the religious basis for the way of nonviolence. Without a spiritual basis at its heart, the way of nonviolence would simply be another inadequate "method," too weak to support man's deepest hopes and not lofty enough to enable anyone to transcend the ordinary in the pursuit of a lasting and durable peace.

Merton was fully aware that the commitment to truth and the way of nonviolence which he advocated were perhaps the most exacting of all forms of struggle. This was so because his approach demanded first of all that one be ready to suffer evil and even face the threat of death without violent retaliation. It was also exacting because it excluded mere transient self-interest and even political interests from its considerations. In a very real sense Merton held that one who practices nonviolent resistance ". . . must commit himself not to the defense of his own interests or even those of a particular group; he must commit himself to the defense of objective truth and right and, above all, of men."[10]

In Merton's mind the pursuit of peace was something total, requiring all of one's energies. "Peace," he wrote, "demands the most heroic labor and the most difficult sacrifice. It demands greater heroism than war."[11] Because of these all-encompassing demands, the philosophy of nonviolence is more a way of life and a life-style and not merely a theory or abstraction. It demands the greatest fidelity to truth and the most rigorous purity of conscience.

The humanistic basis of Christian nonviolence does not presuppose division in man but is built upon the basic unity of man. Its aim is the "healing and reconciliation of man with himself, man the person and man the human family."[12] Because it aims at the good of all people and the objective and universal truth, the fully consistent practice of nonviolence "demands a solid metaphysical and religious basis both in being and in God."[13] For the Christian the basis of nonviolence is "the Gospel message of salvation for *all men* and of the Kingdom of God to which all are summoned."[14]

The religious foundation of nonviolence, Merton said, was faith in Christ the Redeemer and obedience to his demand to love and manifest himself in us by a certain manner of acting in the world and in relation to other people.[15] This existential approach to religion and spirituality as something to be lived and practiced, as well as believed, is another important characteristic of the way of nonviolence involving the whole person.

Merton thought that the new mode of life which Jesus preached was proclaimed most boldly in the Sermon on the Mount. He considered the beatitudes to be the theological foundation of Christian nonviolence, especially, "Blessed are the poor in spirit . . . blessed are the meek."[16] The "poor in spirit" for Merton were the humble of the earth, the oppressed who have no human weapons to rely on and who nevertheless resist evil. In other words, they seek justice in the power of truth and of God not by the power of man. This approach refrains from self-assertion and from violent aggression, because it sees all things in the light of the Good News preached by Jesus and the final fulfillment in the age to come. There is a definite eschatological quality about Christian meekness, peace, and nonviolence which enables people to endure the suffering asked of them during this lifetime.

Alongside this eschatological dimension of Christian nonviolence is a belief in the dynamic of growth which is so much a part of the Kingdom of God, a dynamic made clear in the parables of the mustard seed and of the yeast. This is the dynamism of patient and secret growth in belief that out of the smallest, weakest, and most insignificant seed the greatest tree will come. Merton recalled that the early Church and the record of the apostles and martyrs vividly testified to the inherent and mysterious dynamism. He stated that Christian nonviolence today must be rooted in this same consciousness and faith.

He considered this aspect of Christian nonviolence extremely important, because it gave the key to a proper understanding of meekness. This understanding accepts being "with strength" and is not meekness arising out of quietism, defeatism, or false passivity, but in "trusting in the strength of the Lord of truth."[17] Indeed, he often repeated that Christian nonviolence was nothing, ". . . if not first of all a formal profession of faith in the Gospel message that the Kingdom has been established and that the Lord of truth is risen and reigning over his kingdom, defending the deepest values of those who dwell in it."[18]

Christian peace was considered since the earliest days of the Church as an eschatalogical gift of the Risen Christ, which could not be achieved by any ethical or political program. In keeping with the Scriptures, Merton believed that Christian peace is in fact a fruit of the Spirit and a sign of the Divine Presence in the world.[19]

True peace comes from within a person who is at peace with himself, a person unified and in harmony with his ground of being. This level of awareness and inner unity is reached through contemplation and contemplative solitude. All Christians are called to work for this contemplative awareness which leads to peacefulness, because all Christians by their very adoption as sons and daughters of God are, in Christ, peacemakers. Christians are called to imitate Christ, Merton contended, for instead of defending himself with twelve legions of angels, Christ allowed himself to be nailed to the cross and died praying for his executioners.

The duty of the Christian peacemaker is not to be confused with a kind of quietistic inertia that is indifferent to injustice. It does not accept any disorder, compromise with error and evil, or give in to every pressure in order to maintain peace at any price. Instead, the Christian peacemaker is one who devotes himself totally to the pursuit of peace by positive and energetic means.

Merton was fond of quoting Cardinal Suenens, who when speaking to the United Nations, compared *Pacem in Terris* to a symphony with the leitmotif: "Peace among all peoples requires: truth as its foundation, justice as its rule, love as its driving force, liberty as its atmosphere."[20]

With the meekness preached by Christ in the Sermon on the Mount, the tactic of nonviolence becomes a tactic of love. It is a tactic of love which seeks the salvation and redemption of the opponent, not his castigation, humiliation, and defeat. It does not give in to error and compromise but resists evil and injustice totally, but always with the hope of "winning over" or converting the adversary. This religious dimension of Merton's nonviolence is one of its most demanding aspects, one which calls for a great purity of intention and clear motivation.

Merton said that a "pretended nonviolence" which seeks to defeat and humiliate the adversary is little more than a confession of weakness. True nonviolence is totally different from this, and needless to say, much more difficult. True nonviolence ". . . strives to operate without hatred, without hostility, and without resentment. It works without aggression, taking the side of the good that it is able to find already present in the adversary."[21] While this may be easy to state, it is not at all easy to put into practice, especially when the adversary is aroused to a bitter and violent defense of an injustice he believes to be inflicted upon himself. While this may be true, it should not dissuade or hinder one from taking up the practice of nonviolence, indeed, it should persuade us to accept it all the more seriously and deeply.

The nonviolence advocated by Merton was philosophical and religious; it was a rigorous nonviolence demanding the commitment of the whole person, in a world replete with war and violence. He firmly believed that the cause of nonviolence had to be the Christian alternative to war, and he struggled constantly to awaken Christians to their proper vocation as peacemakers.

Merton undoubtedly has been one of the greatest influences upon the Catholic Peace Movement in the United States and upon its many manifestations. Numerous Merton Centers for the Study of Peace have appeared across the country. Many colleges and universities have courses on Merton and incorporate his thought into courses dealing with peace studies. Dozens of books, dissertations, and theses have appeared each year dealing with some aspect of Merton's fertile thought. The far-reaching aspects of his influence certainly extend to the Bishops of the United States, for many of the challenges that he issued and re-evaluations that he stimulated were discussed and adopted by the National Conference of Catholic Bishops in the final years of the 1960s and the early 1970s. Particularly noteworthy in this regard were the formal statements supporting conscientious objection on the basis of being a Catholic, statements deploring the Vietnam conflict and against war in general, and numerous pastorals showing the futility and immorality of the arms race. The recent major pastoral by the U.S. bishops on war and peace, *The Challenge of Peace*, echoes many of the sentiments of Merton.

James A. Hickey, Archbishop of Washington, D.C., issued on June 3, 1982, the pastoral letter "Nuclear Weapons, Moral Questions: A Pastoral Call to Peacemaking." This statement was an invitation to the Catholic community of Washington to prayer, reflection, and study . . . on the moral dimensions of nuclear weapons in light of Catholic teaching. In the pastoral Archbishop Hickey emphatically stated: "Each of us is called to be a peacemaker; this is not an optional commitment. . . . We approach this task of peacemaking recognizing both its complexity and its urgency. Peacemaking is not some peripheral cause, it is required of each of us."[22]

John Cardinal Krol, Archbishop of Philadelphia, in testimony before a congressional committee on the SALT II treaty, on September 6, 1979, spoke just as strongly. Cardinal Krol stated that the primary moral imperative is to prevent any use of nuclear weapons under any conditions, and that the possession of nuclear weapons in the American policy of deterrence be used to make progress on arms limitation and reductions. He then said that it is imperative for the superpowers to pursue meaningful arms limitation aimed at substantial reductions and real disarmament. Cardianl Krol ended by stating that the "phasing out altogether of nuclear deterrence and the threat of mutual assured destruction must always be the goal of our efforts."[23]

The seed has been sown and the dialogue has been opened in such a way that peacemaking can never fully be stifled or closed again. A person may elect not to work actively for peace, but since the searing commentary and challenge of Thomas Merton, it is extremely difficult to ignore it or our responsibility toward building and working for peace. Initiating such a dialogue between man and his conscience on issues which vitally involve his life is a formidable task. It was one which Merton undertook with characteristic fervor, and one which he relentlessly pursued first throughout his own life, and then in the lives of others. It is a pursuit desperately needed today in the midst of a world fraught with wars and conflicts, threats of a nuclear holocaust, and yet full of untold possibilities for good and peace.

If we are to live as Christians, if we are to live as Americans, then we must confront the reality of war and our nation's stance toward war, armament, and nuclear weapons. We must closely examine our national policies toward arms sales and nuclear stockpiling. It is not an easy task; it is charged with emotion, false security, and fear. It is a complex issue, involving our responsibilities as Americans and as Christians. Our obligation as Christians is clear—we are called to be peacemakers—nothing less will do. As Americans we have the potential to implement that call. Do we have the courage?

We must, as Merton encouraged, begin to seriously formulate and believe in nonviolent alternatives to war and violence for solving conflicts. We must begin to do this on an individual and personal level, as a community, as a Church, and as a nation. The way of nonviolence, stemming from contemplation, as we have presented it here, is one of the best ways that seems to be realistic and retains the bold idealism so necessary in such an undertaking. It is totally demanding, all-encompassing, and without compromise. It involves the whole person in all one's varied dimensions and facets. It touches every aspect of life, and all those we touch.

This is the challenge of Thomas Merton to the modern world of the

1980s. This is his call and plea for sanity and holiness. We have his life as our example, his writing as our guide, his call for contemplation as our basis, and his nonviolence as our way. May we not fall short of the task or shirk the responsibility. Peace is something which must be shared if experienced, given away if received, and worked for if desired. May we not only accept the responsibility and pursue the task, but work creatively and tirelessly for the goal which requires nothing less than our total self and commitment—PEACE.

June 2, 1983
Merion Mercy Campus
Merion Station, Pennsylvania

Epilogue

We cannot stand idly by.

As a faith community, as American citizens, we cannot stand idly by, as our country prepares for nuclear war and acts as though such a war were inevitable and winnable. Thomas Merton called his journal after such a period of silent watching, "Conjectures of a Guilty Bystander." What would we call ours?

I have tried especially in the last fourteen years as Archbishop of Philadelphia, the City of Brotherly Love, to spread the message of peace that rings so clearly from the Gospels and from our recent Popes. In public statements across the country, I have tried to warn of the dangers of the arms race—the single biggest and most dangerous moral problem of our day! I have talked of the horrible inequity of spending between military weapons and research and the poor and needy people in our own country. I have warned of the immorality of the arms build-up which only serves to heighten the risks of war and of the foolish talk about "when" it will take place and "how many" will survive.

My words have helped to raise the popular level of awareness about the dangers of nuclear weapons and nuclear war. Perhaps we need someone like Thomas Merton to increase and maintain a high level of concern about the threat of a nuclear war. Merton is certainly a contemporary American man of peace—worthy of attention and action.

Thomas Merton's way of nonviolence, as described here by Fr.

Givey, is a promising alternative to the traditional responses to war and conflict, namely, more war and conflict.

Father writes inspiringly about Merton who wrestles with God, himself and his country, but who was ultimately true to all three. Merton appeals to many today, especially the young, because he experienced the questions, the ambiguities, the dilemmas, and the crises that so many young people face today. He gives an example of one who faced these questions honestly and responded in a positive and Christian fashion. He protested, but he did so positively. His entrance into the Trappist monastery was his protest against the evils of society and his total acceptance of God and his Church. In the course of a few years that quiet protest was heard around the world, and still is being heard today.

Merton's writings on war and violence and racism are given here clearly and concisely—as a challenge to the American Catholic Church and the American Catholic people. I would like to resound that challenge and again send it forth for all to heed, "for all who have ears to hear, let them hear." This way of nonviolence, as Fr. Givey calls it, this challenge of Thomas Merton, is the challenge and the way of the Beatitudes, it is the way of Jesus Himself.

Pope Paul vi on October 4, 1965, personally told the General Assembly of the United Nations, "No more war, war never again . . . Let the weapons fall from your hands." Ten years later his representative told the same group at the United Nations, "The arms race must be condemned unreservedly. . . . This mad arms race will maintain a false peace, a false security. It will become an end rather than the means . . . it will be a perversion of peace." How sadly true these words have come to be.

Our own beloved Pope John Paul ii has never ceased to preach against the horrors of war. From Auschwitz to Nagasaki, from London to Argentina, in our own City of Brotherly Love, he has pleaded with world leaders, especially of the superpowers, to work for peace, to believe in peace, to be willing to sacrifice for peace. Peace and justice have been his message around the world. I, too, restate the Pope's plea for peace, for more effort to work for peace and make peace a possibility.

September 6, 1979, I testified before a congressional committee on SALT II and said that our primary moral imperative was to prevent any use of nuclear weapons. I stated that the possession of nuclear weapons could be tolerated only to make progress in arms reduction and limitations. I ended the testimony by stating that the ultimate goal must always be the phasing out altogether of nuclear deterrence and the threat of mutual assured destruction.

The American bishops have clearly stated the moral principles on issues of war and peace. We as Americans and Catholics, however, cannot stand idly by—we must make our voices heard. We cannot be like the Apostles who ran and hid while Jesus was being taken to Calvary; we cannot be afraid to be seen and counted. We are called to be peacemakers. We must be willing to work, sacrifice and strive to build peace in our society and in our great country. Thomas Merton has given us a start, a challenge and a way—the way of nonviolence. Let us take it, for it is the way of peace, the way of Jesus Himself.

John Cardinal Krol
Archbishop of Philadelphia

Notes

Prologue

1 Cf. John Eudes Bamberger, "The Monk," p. 46 in *Thomas Merton, Monk: A Monastic Tribute*, ed. Brother Patrick Hart (New York: Doubleday, Image Books, 1974).

Foreword

1 Monica Furlong, *Merton. A Biography* (San Francisco: Harper & Row, Publishers. 1980), p. 264.

2 *Ibid.*, p. xiii.

3 *Ibid.*, p. 320.

4 J. Brian Benestad and Francis J. Butler (eds.), *A Compendium of Statements of the United States Catholic Bishops on the Political and Social Order, 1966–1980* (Washington: United States Catholic Conference. 1981), p. 78.

Chapter I

1 Thomas Merton, *The Seven Storey Mountain* (New York: New American Library, 1963) p. 314.

2 Thomas Merton, *Contemplation in a World of Action* (New York: Doubleday, 1965) pp. 143–44.

3 Thomas Merton, "Is the World a Problem? Ambiguities of a Secular," *The Commonweal* 84 (June 3, 1956) 305.

4 Thomas Merton, *The Sign of Jonas* (New York: Harcourt, Brace, 1956) p. 322.

5 James T. Baker, *Thomas Merton: Social Critic* (Lexington: University of Kentucky Press, 1971) p. 33.

6 Various terms have been used to describe this change in Merton. James Baker, in "The Social Catalyst," *Continuum* 7 (Summer 1969) 259, speaks of a "Startling change in attitude," and in *Thomas Merton: Social Critic*, p. 33, he refers to Merton's "Dramatic change during the 1950s." Frank Dell'Isola, in "A Journey to Gethsemani," *Cross and Crown* VIII (1956) 397, writes of a "great change," "a new Merton." Daniel Callahan, in "Unwordly Wisdom," *Commentary* XXXIX (April 1965) 92, talks about a "different, and perhaps new, Merton."

7 Cf. Matthew Kelly, "Letter from Gethsemani," *Monastic Exchange* I (1969) 87; Sarah Lansdell, "In Search of Thomas Merton," *The Courier-Journal and Times Magazine* (Dec. 7, 1969) 54. Both authors speak of an apparent contradiction between Merton's orientation and love for the solitary and his love for people and the world.

8 Tarcisius Connor, "Merton, Monastic Exchange and Renewal," *Monastic Exchange* I (1969) 2.

9 Thomas Merton, "The Monk Today," *Latitudes*, II (Spring 1968) 13.

10 John J. Higgins, *Thomas Merton on Prayer* (Garden City, N.Y.: Doubleday, 1973), p. 16.

11 Dennis Q. McInerny, *Thomas Merton: The Man and His Work* (Washington: Cistercian Publishing, 1974), p. 59.

12 Thomas Merton, *New Seeds of Contemplation* (New York: New Directions, 1961), p. 80.

13 See Naomi Burton, in her Forward to *My Argument with the Gestapo: A Macaronic Journal,* by Thomas Merton (New York: Doubleday, 1969), p. 8. Likewise, Alice Mayhew, in "Merton Against Himself," *The Commonweal* XCI (Oct. 17, 1969) 71, says of Merton's interests: "In a number of ways he seems to come full circle, and in others one can see a straightforward and exciting line."

14 Gerald Twomey (ed.), *Thomas Merton: Prophet in The Belly of a Paradox* (New York: Paulist Press, 1978): see especially, James H. Forest, "Thomas Merton's Struggle with Peacemaking," pp. 15–79.

15 See Elena Malits, *The Solitary Explorer: Thomas Merton's Transforming Journey* (San Francisco: Harper & Row, 1980), Preface, pp. ix–xiii, where Malits constantly refers to Merton's life as a "journey" of constant conversion and "relentless discovery."

16 Thomas Merton, "First and Last Thoughts: An Author's Preface," p. 13, in Thomas McDonnell (ed.), *A Thomas Merton Reader* (New York: Doubleday, 1974).

17 *Ibid.* p. 16.

18 Thomas Merton, *The Sign of Jonas* (New York: Doubleday Image Books, 1952), p. 11.

19 John Eudes Bamberger, "The Cistercian," *Continuum* 7 (Summer 1969) 229. Cf. also, Charles Dumont, "A Contemplative at the Heart of the World," *Lumen Vitae* 24 (Dec. 1969) 633–46. In a similar vein, Naomi Burton Stone, in "I Shall Miss Thomas Merton," *Cistercian Studies* 4 (1969) 221, speaks of the tension within Merton of "reconciling his real need for seclusion and his real need to give himself to people."

20 Raymond Bailey, *Thomas Merton on Mysticism* (New York: Doubleday, 1975), p. 207.

21 John H. Findlay, *Hegel, A Re-Examination* (New York: Collier, 1962), p. 150.

22 Cf. R. N. Carew Hunt, *The Theory and Practice of Communism* (Baltimore: Pelican Books, 1971), p. 38.

23 Many of Merton's articles, poems, and letters published posthumously have shed light on the direction of his thought during his later years. Recent biographical works based upon previously unavailable sources have likewise helped in tracing Merton's development; see, for example, George Woodcock, *Thomas Merton: Monk and Poet, A Critical Study* (Vancouver, British Columbia: Douglas & McIntyre Ltd., 1978); and Monica Furlong, *Merton: A Biography* (San Francisco: Harper & Row, Publishers, 1980).

24 Bailey, *Thomas Merton on Mysticism*, p. 188.

25 *Ibid.*, p. 189.

26 S. Fitzgerald, "Merton's Progress," *New Republic* CXXVIII (Feb. 3, 1953) 20.

27 *Ibid.*, p. 20.

28 Thomas Merton, "Letter to Friends" (Summer 1967), unpublished. The Merton Studies Center, Louisville, Kentucky.

29 Thomas Merton, *Seeds of Destruction* (New York: Farrar, Straus and Giroux, 1961), pp. 170–71.

30 Thomas Merton, *Raids on the Unspeakable* (New York: New Directions, 1966), p. 159. In tracing Merton's prophetic calling Twomey notes that the "essential paradox of Merton was that he was able to occupy himself critically with the world only after he found his own solitude," in Twomey, *Thomas Merton: Prophet in the Belly of a Paradox*, p. 8.

31 Thomas Merton, "A Buyer's Market for Love?" *Ave Marie* CIV, no. 26 (Dec. 24, 1966) 27.

32 Thomas Merton, *New Seeds of Contemplation*, p. 53.

33 Thomas Merton, "Letter to Lorraine," *Blue Print* X (Fort Lee, New Jersey: Holy Angels Academy, June 1964) 13. This letter was written to a high school girl who had asked Merton, "How can a Catholic writer have the greatest possible influence on his public?"

34 McInerny, *Thomas Merton: The Man and His Work*, p. 77.

35 Bailey, *Thomas Merton on Mysticism*, p. 156.

36 Cf. Thomas Merton, *Conjectures of a Guilty Bystander* (Garden City, New York: Doubleday Image, 1966), p. 110ff Thomas Merton, *Faith and Violence: Christian Teaching and Christian Practice* (Notre Dame, Indiana: University of Notre Dame Press, 1968, p. 47ff and p. 69ff; and Thomas Merton, "A Martyr for Peace and Unity," in Gordon C. Zahn (ed.), *Thomas Merton on Peace* (New York: McCall Publishing Co., 1971), pp. 139–40; rev. ed., printed under the title *The Nonviolent Alternative* (New York: Farrar, Straus and Giroux, 1980).

37 Thomas Merton, "Letter to An Innocent Bystander," in Merton, *Raids on the Unspeakable*, p. 53–64.

38 *Ibid.*, p. 59. It is interesting to note similar warnings by the neo-Marxist, Ernst Bloch, who calls himself "an atheist for God's sake," when he writes to the world's intellectuals to creatively and actively plan for the future. Bloch wrote that one of the functions of utopias (which for him symbolize man's hope for the future) is to "facilitate the engagement of the intellectual in the construction of a better world." Cf. Ernst Bloch, *Prinzip Hoffnung* IV (Berlin: 1959), pp. 164ff., and Pierre Furter, "Utopias and Marxism According to Bloch," *Philosophy Today* XIV, no. 4/4 (Winter 1964) 564.

39 Cf. Thomas Merton, *The Ascent to Truth* (London: Burns & Oates, 1951) on St. John of the Cross; and Thomas Merton, *Exile Ends in Glory* (Milwaukee: Bruce, 1948) on Mother Berchmans.

40 Thomas Merton, *Life and Holiness* (New York: Doubleday, 1964), p. 24.

41 Twomey, *Thomas Merton: Prophet in the Belly of a Paradox*, pp. 9-10. Nouwen notes too that "precisely because Merton had discovered . . . non-violent compassion . . . could he in a real sense be a monk . . . who unmasks through his criticism the illusions of a violent society and who wants to change the world in spirit and truth," Henri J. M. Nouwen, *Pray to Live: Thomas Merton, Contemplative Critic* (Notre Dame, Indiana: Ave Marie Press, 1970), p. 66.

42 Thomas Merton, "Called Out of Darkness," *Sponsa Regis* XXXIII (Nov., 1961) pp. 66-67.

43 Merton, *New Seeds of Contemplation*, p. 31.

44 *Ibid.*, p. 36.

45 Merton, *Conjectures of a Guilty Bystander*, p. 157. Baker describes this particular incident as "a mystical experience in his new confrontation with the world" (cf. Baker, *Thomas Merton: Social Critic*, p. 37).

46 Baker, *Thomas Merton: Social Critic*, p. 38.

47 Thomas Merton, "The Challenge of Responsibility," *Saturday Review* XLVII (Feb. 13, 1965) pp. 28-30.

48 Thomas Merton, *Disputed Questions* (New York: Farrar, Straus and Cudahy, 1960), Preface, p. vii.

49 *Ibid.*, p. ix.

50 *Ibid.*, p. 31.

51 *Ibid.*, p. 6.

52 *Ibid.*, p. 10.

53 *Ibid.*, p. 65.

54 Thomas Merton, "Christianity and Mass Movements," *Cross Currents* IX, No. 3 (Summer 1969) p. 201.

55 *Ibid.*, p. 202.

56 Merton, *New Seeds of Contemplation*, p. 54.

57 Merton, *Conjectures of a Guilty Bystander*, p. 238.

58 Merton, "Christianity and Mass Movements," 211.

59 Merton, *Conjectures of a Guilty Bystander*, pp. 82–3.

60 Frederic J. Kelly, *Thomas Merton on Social Responsibility* (Garden City, N.J.: Doubleday, 1974), p. 179ff.

61 Thomas Merton, "Peace: A Religious Responsibility," in Gordan Zahn (ed.), *Thomas Merton on Peace*, p. 117.

62 "Pastoral Constitution on the Church in the Modern World" in *The Documents of Vatican* II (ed.) Walter M. Abbott (New York: America Press, 1966), #38, p. 236.

63 Thomas Merton, *The Monk: Prophet to Modern Man*, Tape 9B, *The Thomas Merton Tapes* (ed.) Norm Kramer (Chappaqua, New York: Electronic Paperbacks, 1972).

64 Merton, *Raids on the Unspeakable*, p. 75.

65 Thomas Merton, "Final Integrationa Toward a Monastic Therapy" *Monastic Studies* 6 (All Saints, 1968) p. 98.

66 Charles Dumont, "A Contemplative at the Heart of the World," *Lumen Vitae* 24 (Dec. 1969) p. 634.

Chapter II

1 Merton, *New Seeds of Contemplation*, p. 1.

2 Thomas Merton, *The New Man* (New York: Farrar, Straus and Cudahy, 1961), p. 11.

3 The theme for the Forty-first International Eucharistic Congress held in Philadelphia, August 1–8, 1976, was "The Hungers of the Human Family," and stressed the basic hungers that man experiences: hunger for God and truth, hunger for freedom and justice, hunger for understanding and peace. Like Merton's approach the Congress stressed the nature of person as hunger. Cf. Sister Vilma Seelaus, "Hunger for God" Tape #1, (Albany, New York: Clarity Publishing, 1975).

4 Merton, *The New Man*, p. 6.

5 Merton, *New Seeds of Contemplation*, p. 7.

6 *Ibid.*, p. 51.

7 Merton, *Raids on the Unspeakable*, p. 17.

8 Merton, *Conjectures of a Guilty Bystander*, p. 158.

9 Thomas Merton, "Poetry and the Contemplative Life," *The Commonweal* XLVI (July 4, 1957) p. 281.

10 Thomas Merton, *Mystics and Zen Masters* (New York: Dell 1967), p. viii.

11 Thomas Merton, "The Inner Experience," p. 131 (unpublished, in the Thomas Merton Collection at Bellarmine College, Louisville, Kentucky). Although this entire work has not been published, lengthly parts of it are printed in Bailey, *Thomas Merton on Mysticism* (cf. pp. 134–187).

12 Thomas Merton, "Notes for a Philosophy of Solitude," p. 178, in Merton, *Disputed Questions*, pp. 177–207.

13 James Finley, *Merton's Palace of Nowhere: A Search for God Through Awareness of the True Self* (Notre Dame, Indiana: Ave Marie Press, 1978), p. 44.

14 Dom Aelred Graham, "Thomas Merton: A Modern Man in Reverse" *Atlantic Monthly* 191:1 (Jan. 1953) 70–74; John Logan, "Babel Theory," *The Commonweal* LXVI (July 4, 1957) 357–58; and Daniel J. Callahan, "Unwordly Wisdom," *Commentary* XXXIX (April 1965) 92–94; all of whom basically disagreed with Merton's philosophy of contemplation.

15 Thomas Merton, *No Man Is An Island* (New York: Harcourt, Brace, 1955), p. 47.

16 Merton, *Raids on the Unspeakable*, p. 15.

17 Merton, *Disputed Questions*, p. 188.

18 Merton, *No Man Is An Island*, pp. 183–85.

19 Merton, *Disputed Questions*, p. 192.

20 Merton, *Faith and Violence*, p. 215.

21 Thomas Merton, *Contemplative Prayer* (New York: Herder and Herder, 1969), p. 118.

22 Merton, *New Seeds of Contemplation*, p. 5.

23 See Finley, *Merton's Palace of Nowhere*, for a good analysis of Merton's thought on true and false self and the many psychological dimensions of the quest for self through contemplation.

24 Merton, *Faith and Violence*, p. 217.

25 Merton, *The New Man*, p. 15.

26 Thomas Merton, *Gandhi on Non-Violence* (New York: New Directions, 1964), p. 6.

27 Merton, *Disputed Questions*, p. x.

28 Merton, *Life and Holiness*, p. 28.

29 *Ibid.*, pp. 38–42. The 1971 Synod of Bishops formally declared this position in its forceful document, "Justice in the World" (Rome: *Typis Polyglottis Vaticanis*, 1971), in which the Synod recommended education in justice and the Christian's involvement in action for social justice (cf. pp. 18–22).

30 Merton, *Conjectures of a Guilty Bystander*, p. 141.

31 Thomas Merton, "Renewal in Monastic Education," *Cistercian Studies* 3 (Third Quarter 1968) 247–52.

32 Merton, *Seeds of Contemplation*, pp. 52–54.

33 Thomas Merton, "Final Integration," p. 224, in Thomas Merton, *Contemplation in a World of Action* (New York: Doubleday, 1965). Merton's views on aesthetics and creativity in art and literature stem from his notion of the finally integrated person: see, Thomas Merton, "The Catholic and Creativity," *The American Benedictine Review* XI (Sept. Dec., 1960) 197–213.

34 *Ibid.*, p. 226. Much of Merton's thinking on final integration of the personality is parallel to that of the humanistic psychoanalysis of Erich Fromm and the existential psychotherapy of Viktor Frankl. He cites an interesting book by Dr. Reza Arasteh, *Final Integration in the Adult Personality* (Leiden: Brill, 1965), in which Dr. Arasteh developed and deepened the ideas of Fromm and Frankl and incorporated them into his own theories with material borrowed from the mystical tradition of Persian Sufism: cf. Merton, *Contemplation in a World of Action*, pp. 222–25.

35 *Ibid.*, p. 222.

36 *Ibid.*, p. 204.

37 Thomas Merton, "Christian Culture Needs Oriental Wisdom," *The Catholic World* CXCV (May 1962) 78.

38 Merton, *Mystics and Zen Masters*, p. 45.

39 Thomas Merton, "The New Consciousness," in Thomas Merton, *Zen and the Birds of Appetite* (New York: New Directions, 1968), pp. 15ff. Merton explains here how this situation evolved. See also, Thomas Merton, "The Zen Revival," *Continuum* 1, (Winter, 1964) 523–38.

40 *Ibid.*, p. 4. See also the anthology of Merton's basic writings on Zen, *Thomas Merton on Zen* (London: Sheldon Press, 1976); and

William F. Healy, *The Thought of Thomas Merton Concerning the Relationship of Christianity and Zen* (Rome: Pontificia Studiorum Universitas, A S. Thoma Aq. in Urbe, 1975), especially pp. 22–29.

41 *Ibid.*, p. 22. Cf. Malits, *The Solitary Explorer*, pp. 111–13.

42 *Ibid.*, p. 22. There results, as a consequence of this approach, a great need to break out of this imprisonment to embrace the "other." Merton wondered whether it was really possible for the Cartesian consciousness to attain a genuine encounter cf. *ibid.*, p. 23.

43 Merton, *Faith and Violence*, p. 279.

44 Merton, *Zen and the Birds of Appetite*, p. 32.

45 Gordon C. Zahn, "Maritain, Merton and Non-Violence," *Cross Currents* XXXI, no. 3 (Fall, 1981) 297.

46 Merton, *Mystics and Zen Masters*, p. 14. See also, Paul F. Knitter, "Merton's Eastern Remedy for Christianity's Anonymous Dualism," *Cross Currents* XXXI, no. 3 (Fall 1981) 285ff.

47 *Ibid.*, 17.

48 *Ibid.*, 18. See also, Alvin W. Hergott, "Thomas Merton and the Image of Man," unpublished master's thesis, University of Saskatchewan, Regina, 1971, for an interesting presentation of Merton's views on Western consciousness and an analysis of Merton's "alternative consciousness."

49 *Ibid.*, pp. 207ff.

50 Merton, *Zen and the Birds of Appetite*, p. 45. In an article about former Governor Jerry Brown of California, in which the young Governor is called a "Zen Jesuit," the author describes Zen as "the emptying of self and the radical perception of the unity of being. . . . Zen is primarily—in Western terms—an *ascesis*, a way." The article makes two references to Governor Brown's approach to society and government as being "in the tradition of Thomas Merton." Cf. Kevin Starr, "Jerry Brown: The Governor as Jesuit," *City of San Francisco* (Jan. 20, 1975) 10, no. 28, 17–22.

51 McInerny, *Thomas Merton: The Man and His Work*, p. 96.

52 Malits, *The Solitary Explorer* (cf. "A Poor Pilgrim," pp. 98–119).

53 *Ibid.*, p. 108.

Chapter III

1 Merton, *Fatih and Violence*, Part III.

2 McDonnell (ed.), *A Thomas Merton Reader*, p. 276.

3 Merton, *Seeds of Contemplation*, p. 66.

4 *Ibid.*, p. 66.

5 McDonnell, *A Thomas Merton Reader*, p. 276.

6 Merton, *Faith and Violence*, p. 92.

7 Merton, *Seeds of Destruction*, p. 116.

8 Pope John xxiii, *Pacem In Terris* (Boston: Daughters of St. Paul, 1963), N.C.W.C. translation, No. 122; quoted in Merton, *Seeds of Destruction*, p. 116.

9 Pope Paul vi, "On Disarmament," in *The Catholic Standard and Times*, Philadelphia (June 15, 1978), p. 6.

10 *Ibid.*, p. 6.

11 Pope John Paul ii, "To Reach Peace, Teach Peace," reprinted by *Pax Christi, USA* (Chicago, Illinois: Pax Christi Newsletter Documentation, 1979), p. 4.

12 *Ibid.*

13 *Ibid.*, p. 5.

14 John Cardinal Krol, "Arms Race Folly Condemned," in *The Catholic Standard and Times*, Philadelphia (June 28, 1979), p. 13, Joseph Ryan, reporter.

15 *Ibid.*, p. 13. Numerous American bishops have recently publicly denounced the arms race, nuclear war, and arms spending. One of the most publicized cases is that of Archbishop Raymond Hunthausen of Seattle, Washington, who on January 26, 1982, announced that he would refuse to pay 50 percent of his federal income tax in opposition to the nuclear arms race, *National Catholic Reporter*, (Feb. 12, 1982), pp. 42–43.

16 *Ibid.*, p. 13.

17 Merton, *Faith and Violence*, p. 3.

18 *Ibid.* (cf. Ch. I, pp. 3–13).

19 *Ibid.*, p. 4.

20 *Ibid.*, p. 35; cf. Ch. III, "Non-Violence and the Christian Conscience," pp. 30–39.

21 *Ibid.*, p. 4; this is Merton's aim in writing this book.

22 Pope John Paul II has called for just such an investigation since he has called the arms race "a consequence of an ethical crisis that is disrupting society in all its political, social and economic dimensions." In his statement to the United Nations General Assembly's special session on disarmament, delivered on June 11, 1982, by Agostino Cardinal Casaroli, secretary of state, the Pope called for a "ethical renewal." Cf. *The Catholic Standard and Times*, Philadelphia (June 17, 1982) p. 1.

23 Merton, *Faith and Violence*, p. 5. See also, Thomas Merton, "Nuclear War and Christian Responsibility," *The Commonweal* LXXX (Feb. 9, 1962) 510, where he writes that ". . . the use of force does not become moral just because the government and the mass media have declared the cause to be patriotic. The cliché 'My country right or wrong' does not provide a satisfactory theological answer to the moral problems raised by the intervention of American power in all parts of the Third World."

24 *Ibid.*, p. 7.

25 Merton, *Conjectures of a Guilty Bystander*, p. 86.

26 See Merton, *Faith and Violence*, Part III, "From Non-Violence to Black Power," pp. 121–82, and a short summary in Robert Voight, *Thomas Merton, A Different Drummer* (Liguori, Missouri: Liguori Pub., 1974), pp. 63–92.

27 Origen, *Contra Celsum*, III Chadwick t. (New York: Oxford University Press, 1966), p. 133; quoted in Merton, *Seeds of Destruction*, p. 137.

28 Merton, *Seeds of Destruction*, pp. 135–36.

29 *Ibid.*, p. 139.

30 *Ibid.*, p. 139; cf. Origen, *Contra Celsum*, V, p. 33.

31 *Ibid.*, p. 150.

32 *Ibid.*, p. 141. In another place Merton writes, "Prayer and sacrifice must be used as the most effective spiritual weapons in the war against war, and like all weapons, they must be used with deliberate aim: not just with a vague aspiration for peace and security, but against violence and war" cf. Thomas Merton, *The Catholic Worker [Oct. 1961]*, p. 1.

33 *Ibid.*, p. 143. See also, David W. Givey, "Thomas Merton as Peacemaker: The Way of Nonviolence," *Cistercian Studies* (no. 4, 1981) 334.

34 Cf. Dino Bigongiari, "The Political Ideas of St. Augustine," in *The Political Writings of St. Augustine,* (Chicago: Regnery, 1970).

35 Merton, *Seeds of Destruction,* pp. 144–45; see also, Rex Martin, "The Two Cities in Augustine's Political Philosophy," Journal of the History of Ideas XXXIII (April-June, 1972) no. 2, 198–210.

36 Voight, *Thomas Merton: A Different Drummer,* p. 30.

37 *Ibid.*, p. 31.

38 Augustine, Letter 138, quoted in Merton, *Seeds of Destruction,* p. 147.

39 Merton, *Seeds of Destruction,* p. 146.

40 Cf. Austin Fagothey, *Right and Reason, Ethics in Theory and Practice,* (5th ed.), (St. Louis: C. V. Mosby Co., 1973), p. 397, for a good exposition of the traditional theory; and Robert W. Tucker, *Just War and Vatican Council II: A Critique* (New York: The Council on Religion and International Affairs, 1966), for a critical evaluation and definition.

41 Merton, *Seeds of Destruction,* p. 145.

42 Pope John Paul II, *Dives in Misericordia,* printed in *The Catholic Standard and Times,* Philadelphia (Dec. 4, 1980), p. 3.

43 Merton, *Seeds of Destruction,* p. 148.

44 *Ibid.*, p. 152.

45 Merton, "Christian Ethics and Nuclear War," p. 85, in *Thomas Merton on Peace.*

46 Merton, "Nuclear War and Christian Responsibility," p. 512. It is interesting to note how different from Merton's approach is that of Paul Ramsey, whose book, *War and the Christian Conscience* (Durhan, N.C.: Duke University Press, 1961), has the subtitle "How Shall Modern War be Conducted Justly?" Seven years later in the Introduction to his book *The Just War,* (New York: Scribner's, 1969) he still regarded his earlier work as the "fundamental and historical statement of the ethical justification of Christian participation in the use of military force, and of the conditions, tests, and limits of 'just war.' " For a clear and concise analysis of Ramsey's thought on double effect in "just wars" see, Edwin F. O'Brien, *The Origin and Development of Moral*

Principles in the Writings of Paul Ramsey, doctoral diss. (Rome: Pontificia Studiorum Universitas A S. Thoma Aq. in Urbe, 1978), cf. pp. 153–57, 247–53.

47 Merton, "Christianity and Defense in a the Nuclear Age," in *Thomas Merton on Peace,* p. 89.

48 Merton, *Seeds of Destruction,* p. 120.

49 *Time* (March 29, 1982), pp. 10–26.

50 *Ibid.,* p. 10.

51 Merton, "Nuclear War and Christian Responsibility," *The Commonweal* LXXX (Feb. 9, 1962) 512.

52 *Ibid.,* 512.

53 Merton, "Christianity and Defense in the Nuclear Age," reprinted in *Thomas Merton on Peace,* p. 88. The first draft of the national letter by the U.S. Bishops released in June 1982 judges two major aspects of U.S. nuclear deterrence strategy clearly immoral—the use or threat to use nuclear weapons first, and any use or threat of nuclear weapons against civilian populations. The draft seriously questions whether the stringent conditions for a morally justified use of nuclear weapons could ever be met in practice (see *The Catholic Standard and Times* [July 15, 1982], p. 12). Editor's note: The final draft, issued May, 1983, states this even more forcefully.

54 *Ibid.,* p. 89.

55 Merton, "Nuclear War and Christian Responsibility," 511.

56 Merton, "Christianity and Defense in the Nuclear Age," p. 90.

57 Along this line of Merton's thought, John Cardinal Krol, Archbishop of Philadelphia, told the World Synod of Bishops in October, 1971, that the armaments race was not the way to protect human life or foster peace. "On the contrary," Cardinal Krol said, "little by little it aggravates the causes of war." He cited three reasons why the arms race is unjust: it violates the rights of citizens of the nations that are involved in it because of the heavy burden of taxation they must bear; it deprives citizens of poor nations of aid and economic assistance; it offends the rights of all men who may as a result become the victims of some unforeseen disaster and who live always in the fearful shadow of third world war. Cf. *Origins,* Documentary Service (Nov. 4, 1971).

58 Merton, *Seeds of Destruction,* p. 119.

59 *Ibid.,* p. 120.

60 *Ibid.*, p. 121.

61 Merton, "Christianity and Defense," p. 90.

62 Thomas Merton, "Peace: A Religious Responsibility," Ch. 12, p. 125, in *Thomas Merton on Peace.*

63 Gordon Zahn, "An Appreciation," introduction to *Thomas Merton on Peace,* p. xvii, one of the best summaries of Merton's thought on peace.

64 Cf. "Prologue," Brother Patrick Hart, p. x.

65 Pope Pius XII "Christmas Message," 1944, p. 324.

66 Zahn, "An Appreciation," p. xx.

67 The first draft of the pastoral letter of the U.S. Bishops, "The Challenge of Peace: God's Promise and Our Response," representing the work of a five-bishop committee, while it condemns some aspects of U.S. nuclear deterrence policy, it does not condemn outright all possession or production of nuclear weapons or any conceivable use of them. It tolerates a policy of nuclear deterrence, within specified limits, saying it is a moral evil that must be eliminated from the world but cannot be eliminated safely by sudden or completely unilateral action.

68 Merton, *New Seeds of Contemplation,* pp. 122–23.

69 *Ibid.,* p. 122.

70 *Ibid.,* p. 123.

71 David C. Morrison, "Armageddon in Triplicate, Life After Doomsday," *The Commonweal* (July 16, 1982) 398–99.

72 *Ibid.,* p. 399. Morrison adds that such "nuclear survival fantasies are shared by too many policymakers at the highest levels to be dismissed out of hand. Local civil defense planners may be rehearsing the dance of death, but Washington pays the piper."

73 Quoted by Gordon Zahn in "The Peacemaker," *Continuum* 17 (Summer 1969) no. 2, 509. Merton often used this expression.

74 Merton, *Seeds of Destruction,* p. 234. See also, "Gandhi and the One-Eyed Giant," Introduction to Thomas Merton, *Gandhi on Non-Violence* (New York: New Directions, 1965), pp. 1–23.

75 Merton, "Gandhi and the One-Eyed Giant," p. 3. The sacred *dharma* was the duty, law, and virtue of the Indian people. It meant they were to get involved in political life and and collaborate in setting

things right; it is a social virtue stemming from a deeply religious principle within man.

76 *Ibid.*, p. 5.

77 *Ibid.*, p. 6. *Satyagraha* is a term coined by Gandhi. Its root meaning is "holding on to truth," and by extension, resistance bv nonviolent means.

78 *Ibid.*, p. 4.

79 Merton, *Conjectures of a Guilty Bystander*, p. 118.

80 Merton, *Seeds of Destruction*, p. 226.

81 *Ibid.*, p. 231.

82 Cf. Merton, "Gandhi and the One-Eyed Giant," p. 30, where Merton quotes Mohandas K. Gandhi *Non-Violence in Peace and War* (Ahmedabad, India: Navajivan Trust Publishing Co., 1930).

83 Merton, *Gandhi on Non-Violence*, p. 35.

84 Merton, *Conjectures of a Guilty Bystander*, p. 84.

85 Merton, *Seeds of Destruction*, p. 231.

86 *Ibid.*, p. 232.

87 Gandhi, *Non-Violence in Peace and War*, 1–144, quoted by Merton in *Gandhi on Non-Violence*, p. 28.

88 Thomas Merton, "Peace and Revolution: A Footnote from Ulysses," *Peace*, (Fall/Winter, 1968–1969), p. 10.

89 Merton, *Conjectures of a Guilty Bystander*, p. 85.

90 *Ibid.*, p. 85.

91 Merton, "Gandhi and the One-Eyed Giant," p. 12.

92 *Ibid.*, p. 12. Unfortunately, Merton does not develop this theme more thoroughly. He does, however, deal with the "sanity" and "obedience" of Adolf Eichmann in a cynical and searing essay entitled "A Devout Meditation in Memory of Adolf Eichmann," in *Raids on the Unspeakable* (New York: New Directions, 1966), pp. 45–52.

93 St. Thomas, *Summa Theologica*, II, IIae, q. 30, art. 1 and ad. 1.

94 Merton, "Gandhi and the One-Eyed Giant," p. 13.

95 Nouwen, *Pray to Live*, p. 132.

96 Gandhi, *My Non-Violence* (Ahmedabad: India, Navajivan Trust Publishing Co., 1930), pp. 182–83; quoted by Merton in *Conjectures of a Guilty Bystander*, p. 117.

97 Merton, "Gandhi and the One-Eyed Giant," p. 20.

Chapter IV

1 Thomas Merton, "The Challenge of Responsibility," *Saturday Review* XLVII (Feb. 13, 1965) 28–30.

2 Merton, *Seeds of Destruction*, p. 164.

3 *Ibid.*, p. 163.

4 Cf. Thomas Merton, "Is Man a Gorilla With a Gun?" in Merton, *Faith and Violence*, Part II, Ch. 2, pp. 96–105. In this chapter Merton attacks the position of Robert Ardrey, who in his best-selling book, *African Genesis* (New York: Scribners, 1954) contends that man is a born killer, descended from the apes and "fathered by weapons."

5 Merton, *Faith and Violence*, p. 7; see also Niccolò Machiavelli, *The Prince* (New York: Airmont, 1965).

6 Merton, *Seeds of Destruction*, Part III, Ch. I, Section 4, "The Legacy of Machiavelli," p. 152.

7 Machiavelli, *The Prince*, p. 73.

8 Merton, *Seeds of Destruction*, p. 156.

9 *Ibid.*, p. 164.

10 *Ibid.*, p. 165.

11 Pope John XXIII, *Pacem in Terris* (Boston: St. Paul Editions, 1963), no. 138; quoted in *Seeds of Destruction*, p. 166.

12 *Ibid.*, nos. 47 and 48.

13 Merton, *Seeds of Destruction*, p. 168; and *Pacem in Terris*, No. 49.

14 Pope John, *Pacem in Terris*, no. 50.

15 Merton, *Seeds of Destruction*, p. 170.

16 *Ibid.*, p. 171.

17 *Ibid.*, p. 173.

18 *Ibid.*, p. 174.

19 Joseph Pieper, *Guide to St. Thomas* (New York: Mentor-Omega, 1955), p. 120; quoted in *Seeds of Destruction*, p. 177.

20 Merton, *Seeds of Destruction*, p. 178.

21 Cardinal Maurice Roy, "Reflections," delivered on the occasion of the tenth anniversary of the encyclical *Pacem in Terris*, April 11, 1973 (Rome: 1973).

22 Merton, *Conjectures of a Guilty Bystander*, p. 5.

23 Merton, *Contemplation in a World of Action*, p. 24.

24 Merton, "Christianity and Defense in a Nuclear Age," p. 69.

25 Pope John xxiii, *Message of Peace,* "A Special Appeal to World Leaders to Settle Grave International Situations by Peaceful Means," given Sept. 8, 1961, at Vatican City (Boston: St. Paul Editions, 1961), cf. 6.

26 Merton, "Peace: A Religious Responsibility," p. 127.

27 *Ibid.,* cf. pp. 127–28 and p. 109.

28 Merton, *Seeds of Destruction,* p. 96.

29 *Ibid.,* p. 96.

30 Merton, *Faith and Violence,* p. 43.

31 *Ibid.,* p. 44.

32 *Ibid.,* p. 28.

33 *Ibid.,* pp. 27–28.

34 *Ibid.,* p. 31.

35 Baker, "The Social Catalyst," p. 260.

36 Merton, *Faith and Violence,* p. 14.

37 *Ibid.,* p. 14.

38 *Ibid.,* p. 16.

39 *Ibid.,* p. 16.

40 *Ibid.,* p. 16. Merton often emphasized this universal dimension of nonviolence.

41 *Ibid.,* p. 20.

42 *Ibid.,* p. 20.

43 *Ibid.,* pp. 21–26.

44 *Ibid.,* p. 23.

45 Francis X. Meehan, *A Contemporary Social Spirituality* (Maryknoll, New York: Orbis Books, 1982), p. 120.

46 *Ibid.,* p. 121.

47 Voigt, *Thomas Merton,* p. 44.

48 Merton rejoiced at the Second Vatican Council's "Constitution on the Church in the Modern World" which recognized the right of Catholics to refuse to bear arms on the grounds of conscience (cf. no. 79). The American Bishops in 1968 made a strong statement to the same effect. For a fully documented life of Jägerstätter, see Gordon Zahn, *In Solitary Witness* (New York: Holt, Rinehard & Winston, 1964), which Merton Merton frequently refers to in his analysis.

49 Merton, *Faith and Violence,* p. 282.

50 Dietrick Bonhoeffer, *Letters and Papers from Prison* (New York: Macmillan, 1962), p. 14.

51 Alfred Delp, *The Prison Meditations of Father Delp* (New York: Macmillan, 1966).

52 Merton, "A Martyr for Peace and Unity," *Thomas Merton on Peace,* pp. 139–143.

53 *Ibid.* quoted by Merton, p. 142.

54 *Ibid.,* p. 141.

55 Merton, *Faith and Violence,* see pp. 76–86, "Pacifism and Resistance in Simone Weil."

56 The original title was "Let us not start the Trojan War all over again," but it appears in Weil's *Selected Essays* (Oxford: Oxford University Press, 1965), as "The Power of Words." Cf. Merton, *Faith and Violence,* p. 80.

57 Merton, *Faith and Violence,* p. 83.

Chapter V

1 Merton, *The Secular Journal,* pp. 237ff.

2 Merton, *The Seven Storey Mountain,* p. 346.

3 Merton, *A Man in the Divided Sea,* p. 42.

4 Cf. Eldrige Cleaver, *Soul on Ice* (New York: McGraw-Hill, 1968).

5 Merton, *Seeds of Destruction,* pp. 28f and Part One, pp. 3–86.

6 Baker, *Thomas Merton: Social Critic,* p. 99.

7 Merton, "The Shoshoneans," *The Catholic Worker.* XXXIII (June 1967) 5. This is a review of *The Shoshoneans: The People of the Basin-Plateau,* by Edward Dorn (New York: Morrow, 1966), dealing with the white man's treatment of the Shoshonean Indians. See also, "The Shoshoneans," pp. 5–16, in Thomas Merton, *Ishi Means Man,* (Greensboro, North Carolina: Unicorn Press, 1976).

8 Merton, *Seeds of Destruction,* see Part One.

9 *Ibid.,* pp. 33–34.

10 *Ibid.,* p. 34.

11 *Ibid.,* p. 8.

12 *Ibid.*, p. 9.

13 *Ibid.*, p. 65.

14 *Ibid.*, p. 67.

15 *Ibid.*, p. 68.

16 Some examples would be the Montgomery, Alabama, bus boycotts of 1955–56, the sit-ins protesting segregation rides of the 1960s. For a detailed case study of these events, see William R. Miller, *Non-Violence: A Christian Interpretation* (New York: Schocken Books, 1964), especially Ch. 20, "Nonviolence in the Southern United States since 1955," pp. 298–345.

17 Cf. Robert B. Gore, "Nonviolence," in *The Angry Black South* (eds.) Glenford E. Mitchell and William H. Peace iii (New York: Corinth, 1962), pp. 146–47.

18 Merton, *Seeds of Destruction*, p. 45.

19 *Ibid.*, pp. 45–46.

20 *Ibid.*, p. 23.

21 Cf. William M. Kelly, *A Different Drummer* (New York: Dell, 1965); and Merton, *Seeds of Destruction*, pp. 72ff. Merton termed this novel a "parable which spells out some of the deep spiritual implications of the nonviolence battle for full civil rights" (p. 75).

22 James Baldwin, *Go Tell It on the Mountain* (New York: Dell, 1969); see also James Baldwin, *The Fire Next Time* (New York: Dell, 1970).

23 See especially, Martin Luther King, Jr., *Stride Toward Freedom* (New York: Harper and Brothers, 1958, 1963); and *The Trumpet of Conscience* (New York: Harper and Row, 1968).

24 Merton, *Faith and Violence*, p. 121.

25 *Ibid.*, p. 123.

26 *Ibid.*, p. 124.

27 *Ibid.*, p. 128.

28 *Ibid.*, p. 129.

29 *Ibid.*, p. 129.

30 *Ibid.*, p. 143.

31 Dom Helder Camara, *Spiral of Violence*, trans. Della Conling (London: Sheed and Ward, 1971) (cf. pp. 29ff). This book is dedicated, "To The Memory of Gandhi and Martin Luther King."

32 A symposium dealing with violence in American society summa-

rized it thus: "The basic cause of most violent revolt is injustice and inequity, violation of personhood, and symbolic violence" (cf. Thomas Rose ed., *Violence in America* [New York: Random House, 1971], p. 38).

33 Cf. Merton, *Faith and Violence,* pp. 176ff, and Dom Helder Camara, *The Spiral of Violence,* pp. 34ff.

34 José DeBroucker. *Dom Helder Camara: The Violence of a Peacemaker.* (New York: Orbis Books, 1970), p. 31.

35 David W. Givey. "Brazilian Archbishop Denounces 'Internal Colonialism,' " in *The Catholic Standard and Times,* 81, no. 49 (Aug. 5, 1976) p. 31.

36 *Ibid.,* p. 31.

37 Dom Helder Camara, *Church and Colonialism* (London: Sheed and Ward, 1969). This excellent series of essays advocates revolutionary nonviolence in Latin America.

38 King, *Stride Toward Freedom,* pp. 38ff.

39 Baker, *Thomas Merton: Social Critic,* p. 115.

40 Thomas Merton, "Preface," p. vi, in P. R. Regamey, *Non-Violence and the Christian Conscience* (New York: Herder and Herder, 1966); later published in Merton, *Faith and Violence,* pp. 30–39.

41 Baker, *Thomas Merton: Social Critic* (cf. pp. 115–16).

42 Cf. Martin Marty, "Open Letter to Thomas Merton," *National Catholic Reporter,* 3 (Aug. 30, 1967) p. 6; and Thomas Merton, "Thomas Merton Replies to a Perceptive Critic," *National Catholic Reporter,* 3 (Jan. 18, 1968) p. 4.

43 Merton, *Faith and Violence,* pp. 129, 130; see also, Baker, *Thomas Merton Social Critic,* pp. 109–10.

44 Baker, *Thomas Merton: Social Critic,* p. 111.

Conclusion

1 Winthrop Hudson, *Religion in America* (New York: Scribner's, 1965), p. 405.

2 Elena Malits, "Thomas Merton, Symbol and Synthesis," *The Critic* XXXV, no. 3 (Spring 1977) p. 29.

3 James T. Baker, "A Kinsman to So Many," *Commonweal* (April 10, 1981) p. 214.

4 Kelly, *Man Before God*, p. 258.

5 McInerny, *Thomas Merton: The Man and His Work*, p. 121. McInerny writes: "(Merton and Emerson) were ecclectic thinkers, essentially religious writers and dedicated anti-materialists with an innate antipathy toward war and militarism."

6 Baker, "A Kinsman to So Many," p. 215.

7 Merton, *New Seeds of Contemplation*, p. 4.

8 Thomas Merton, "The Universe As Epiphany: The Spirituality of Pierre Teilhard de Chardin," p. 28. Unpublished vol. 6, *Collected Essays*, Thomas Merton Studies Center, Bellarmine College, Louisville, Kentucky.

9 Thomas Merton, *Contemplation in a World of Action*, (New York: Doubleday, 1965), p. 245.

10 Merton, *Faith and Violence*, p. 14.

11 Merton, *Seeds of Destruction*, p. 125.

12 Merton, *Faith and Violence*, p. 15.

13 *Ibid.*, p. 15.

14 *Ibid.*, p. 16.

15 *Ibid.*, p. 16.

16 Matthew 5:3–4, quoted in Merton, *Faith and Violence*, p. 17.

17 Merton, *Faith and Violence*, p. 18.

18 *Ibid.*, p. 19.

19 Galatians 5:22.

20 Address of Cardinal Leo Suenens, Archbishop of Mechelen-Brussels, to the United Nations, (May 13, 1963), quoted in *Seeds of Destruction*, p. 109.

21 Merton, *Conjectures of a Guilty Bystander*, p. 65.

22 Archbishop James A. Hickey, "Nuclear Weapons, Moral Questions: A Pastoral Call to Peacemaking" (Washington, D.C. Office of the Archbishop, June 3, 1982), Prot. No. 49/82, p. 7. Quoted by Archbishop Hickey.

23 *Ibid.*, p. 5.